The Millenium BUG

Gateway to the Cashless Society?

Second Edition

Mark Ludwig

American Eagle Publications, Inc.
Post Office Box 1507
Show Low, Arizona 85902
1998

Copyright 1997, 1998 American Eagle Publications, Inc. All rights reserved. Reproduction without written permission strictly prohibited.

The Millenium Bug: Gateway to the Cashless Society?

Contents

Preface to the Second Edition 3
1. The Millenium Bug 5
2. The Technical Problem in a Nutshell 9
3. Will the Technical Problem Crash the World? 20
4. Doomsday at the Doorstep 28
5. The Great Media Scare 38
6. Risk and Reward Basics 53
7. How the Banking System Works 63
8. The Anatomy of a Banking Collapse 69
9. The Millenium Bug Bank Panic 73
10. A Short Course on National Emergencies 87
11. 1933 and 1999: A Comparison 97
12. Who Wants an Electronic Money System? 111
13. The Politics of Debt 123
14. The Collapsing IRS 133
15. The Great Collapse of 1999 143
16. Electronic Money and Slavery 151
17. Resistance 161
18. The Black Market 175
19. Personal Preparedness 179
20. A Silver Lining? 195
21. Resources 173

Preface to the 2nd Edition

The millenium bug crisis is developing faster than even I imagined it would. Since the time when I wrote the first edition of this book six short months ago, the whole scene has changed significantly. We may not have nearly as much time as I first thought to get ready. coverage of the problem by the press has grown exponentially. Not only that, the stories making their way into print are getting more and more alarming. As a result, the whole scene has changed significantly. We may not have nearly as much time as I first thought to get ready.

As of March, 1998 President Clinton has already issued one executive order concerning the millenium bug, and he's sure to issue more as the crisis intensifies. The media is getting more alarmed too. Last summer, *Newsweek* alone was alerting readers to the possibility of nasty problems. Now many others are chiming in, like *Business Week*, *The Wall Street Journal*, *The Economist*, and many local papers and specialized magazines. Not only that, the stories making their way into print are getting more and more alarming. Things are getting serious. It won't be long before we start seeing stories on the national news, and maybe demands for a national emergency.

Because of the rapid pace of events, I've updated this book to try to keep you up to date on what is happening. I've also expanded the section on personal preparedness.

Preparing for this one event may be the most important thing you do in the next 18 months, and maybe for the rest of your life. It may be the determining factor in whether you, your children, and your children's children live free and prosperous lives, or whether you get chained to a system that will increasingly milk you for all you're worth and leave you poor and despondent.

Finally, I've abandoned my hopes for a political solution. I'm afraid the politicians are just too stupid to figure this one out. The ones who have figured it out are the ones who want it to happen. Still, there may be a silver lining to this dark cloud looming on the horizon.

Mark Ludwig
March 23, 1998

1. The Millenium Bug

You've probably already heard about the "Year 2000 problem," otherwise known as the millenium bug, which is predicted to plague computers the world over on the eve of December 31, 1999/January 1, 2000. The problem stems from the fact that many computer programs save only the last two digits of the date wherever dates are stored. Then they assume that the century is "19" when they retrieve the date. This makes for a potential glitch of worldwide proportions. On New Year's day, 2000, computers using software with this flaw will think it is now the year 1900. Calculations that should be based on the year 2000 will be based on 1900 instead.

Although the potential for technological trouble on January 1, 2000 has started to get publicity, very few people are thinking about how that potential for trouble will affect people's behavior. Imagine millions or billions of people justifiably scared that January 1, 2000 could—just could—be a technological Armageddon. This possibility is far more serious than the technological threat itself. After all, if there is even a 1% chance that your life savings are going to be wiped out on such-and-such a day, you'll do what you can to protect them. If we're talking a stock market crash, you'll call your broker. If we're talking a banking problem, you'll try to beat your neighbors to the bank. Likewise, if computers spell danger on January 1, 2000, you'll do what you can to get out of harm's way.

Think back to the Michelangelo virus scare in 1992. Michelangelo was set to detonate on March 6, 1992. Before the fact, nobody knew whether the virus would hit 5000 computers, 5,000,000 or 50,000,000. There was just no way to know what would happen. The potential for disaster was horrific. The scare only really blossomed about a week before the big event on March 6. *During those few days, people were terrified.* They were imagining the worst, and how it would affect their computers and their lives. Most everybody was willing to do *just about anything* to make sure they were safe. People who sold anti-virus programs made a killing that week.

A similar scare is already brewing up over the millenium bug. However, just as the millenium bug is a problem many orders of magnitude worse than a computer virus, so the scare it creates will be much worse than the Michelangelo scare. Instead of trying to buy an anti-virus program because their hard disk is at risk, people will be trying to convert all of their assets to tangible goods because their life savings and their incomes will be at risk. They may even be moving out of the city because their lives are at risk.

Given the nature of the modern financial system—a highly leveraged system built upon layer after layer of trust—the one thing it cannot cope with is a scare. If even a small fraction of people get scared enough to act, they are fully capable of shutting the entire system down. The banking system will default. Stock and bond markets will collapse. People's life savings will go up in smoke.

Realize that such a scenario is not dependent upon the millenium bug actually wreaking technological havoc. It is only dependent upon a small fraction of people getting worried that it *might* wreak havoc. That is

The Millenium Bug

both more likely and more dangerous than the technological havoc itself.

And when chaos hits our financial system, government intervention is a certainty. The vast majority—who will get stuck in the collapsing system—will demand action. The most likely form which government intervention will take is the conversion to an all-electronic money system.

At first this may be a rather surprising conclusion in the face of a computer catastrophe. We can only understand it if we examine the details of the situation: when the panic will occur, what its likely results will be, the financial pressures currently facing modern governments, and the historical precedents for similar actions.

Remember that the U.S. government solved the banking crisis of 1933 by effectively trapping people in the system with Federal Reserve Notes that were no longer convertible to gold by the average citizen. Don't think they won't trap you again. The laws, executive orders, and precedents put in place at that time provide all of the necessary legal machinery to implement the cashless society in a time of crisis, and the millenium bug is the perfect, made-to-order crisis.

Likewise, the millenium bug may be the catalyst for drastic changes in the way governments are financed. Such a new means of financing is already needed since the bond market has gone about as far as it can. Japanese Prime Minister Hashimoto's July, 1997 threat to sell US securities and buy gold is a thought echoing through the minds of many big holders of government debt. The Treasury and the Federal Reserve are taking this threat seriously. Uncertainties about the millenium bug could drive interest rates up and destroy the bond market. Add to this the fact that the IRS is ready to collapse under the weight of its computer problems, and has no idea how to solve its millenium bug problems.

There should be little wonder that the federal government desperately needs the cashless society to (a) partially default on their debts by suddenly inflating the money supply and (b) implement a new method of funding government. 1933 will be the model for default, when the dollar was devalued overnight from $20/ounce of gold to $35/ounce. In the midst of chaos, the money supply will be up for grabs, and a crisis-induced financial panic will justify whatever is done. For funding, the government will return to milking its own citizens for all of its revenues. In an electronic system, taxes will be collected silently, without the consent, and perhaps without the knowledge of the taxpayer.

Many of us find the idea of a cashless society noxious. Some abhor its invasions of freedom and privacy. Others object for religious reasons. Still others hate the idea of being reduced to slave laborers who can never escape from the system and who are hereditarily bound to spend 80% of their lives working to support the programs and plans of others. To such as these, this book will come as a warning. There is still time to avoid the cashless society—both individually and as a society—but time is quickly running out.

2. The Technical Problem in a Nutshell

We often abbreviate dates without thinking about it. For example, we might write "November the fifteenth, 1967 AD" in any of the following ways:

Nov 15, '67
Nov 15
11-15-1967
11/15/67

It is quite common to use a shorthand for dates day-in and day-out without even thinking about it.

So it should be no big surprise that humans who program computers would abbreviate dates in their programming, especially if they had a good reasons. Back in the early days of computers, when memory space might have cost a dollar per byte or more, abbreviating a date made a lot of sense. The numerical format was used without question, and dropping the century "19" was considered good programming because it saved two bytes of memory. Just as humans understood perfectly well what "11/15/67" meant, computers could be made to understand what it meant, too. So dates were commonly stored in a six-digit format, e.g., the six digits "111567" meant November 15, 1967.

Now, even humans can misinterpret dates that are expressed in abbreviated form if they misunderstand the abbreviation. For example, the date 2-1-97 means February 1, 1997 in the United States. However, in Europe a different convention is used, so 2-1-97 will be read 2 January, 1997. If you don't know about this difference in interpretation, it has the potential to cause great confusion and even trouble. Computers that are programmed to interpret an abbreviated date can be fooled in just the same way. And the two-digit year has just this potential to be misinterpreted in the year 2000.

Of course, back in the 1960's and 1970's, everybody knew that computer technology was proceeding at such a fast pace that these computers would be long gone by the year 2000. By then, we'd have supermachines like HAL in *2001, A Space Oddesy*! And by 1960's standards, we do.

What software developers didn't anticipate is the dynamics of how those old machines would be replaced. At that time, the cost of hardware was astronomical, and the software was relatively cheap. So it was assumed that when new hardware came along, people would buy new hardware and software. However, companies that had made large investments in software, in training employees to use that software, and in creating data with that software didn't want to start all over from scratch. A big selling point for new hardware became the necessity to make the old software work with it, somehow. In the worst case, new software at least had to be able to read the old data. This is called *backward compatibility*.

Simply put, hardware and operating systems that are not backward compatible with the old software have a hard time gaining market share. That's why Microsoft Word for Windows '97 (there we go again with the dates) can read a Word Perfect 5.0 file. That way it can be sold

The Technical Problem in a Nutshell

to somebody who currently uses Word Perfect, and they can still read all of their old documents. That's why your 1997 Pentium-based computer with 64 megabytes of memory running 32-bit Windows can still run a 35 kilobyte DOS-based word processor written in 1981. If that 1997 computer wasn't backward compatible—if it required Windows '97 and a whole new set of software—nobody would buy it. Worse, nobody would write programs for it, because the market wouldn't be there.

This backward compatibility issue has lots to do with the millenium bug. Software that was expected to be obsolete 10 or 20 years ago has in reality lived on far longer than anybody thought it would. And the six digit dates have lived on with it.

Worse, the programmers who knew six digit dates were good programming in the 60's became the professors in the 70's and 80's. They often taught their students to use six digit dates long after the reason for the practice had disappeared. (You can't teach an old dog new tricks.) Likewise, programmers often learned the nitty-gritty details of how to program by looking at older code. College courses might have taught the basics, but the difference between a college-level programmer and an employable one required a knowledge of all kinds of tricks and techniques that could only be learned by looking at the work of other experienced programmers. In the process of becoming expert, novice programmers often learned to use six digit dates. Sometimes they had to, when updating an old program or retro-fitting a new program to handle old data, and the schedule to get the job done was tight, and nobody cared about a petty thing like the dates, so long as the program was up and running next week. Nobody thought much about potential problems this could create later on, and those who did think about it figured the software would be obsolete by then anyhow.

The question is what happens when the century changes? What happens, when the date is no longer *19*XX, but *20*XX? Then the assumption the programmer has made that a six digit date "111567" means "November 15, 1967" is no longer valid. Applying it to the date "012200" will give the date "January 22, 1900" and not "January 22, 2000" as desired.

This simple problem of misinterpretation is the heart of the millenium bug.

To see what kind of a problem it can create, suppose your bank's computer is about to calculate the interest due on your $10,000 savings account from December 15, 1999 through January 15, 2000. If the rate of return is 4%, then one month's interest is 0.3274% or about $32.74. However, if January 15, 2000 is misinterpreted as January 15, 1900, you'll get interest on -99 years, 11 months instead, or -$503,401.48. In short, the computer will wipe out your account and show you are overdrawn by $493,401.48. That would not be a nice surprise for your next bank statement.

If this problem were limited to a few old mainframes running old programs it would be big enough. However, the problem is much bigger than that. Computer programmers inadvertently *trained* people to use a six-digit shorthand for dates. This has created a market force in the software industry. A good programmer knows that forcing a software user to enter an 8-digit date, e.g., "06/15/1997" is irritating to the user after a while, especially if he has lots of dates to enter. The user wants to be able to enter a six-digit date instead. He wants to be able to enter "6/15/97" and let the computer figure the century out. Why does he want that? It saves him two keystrokes. And besides, "plenty of computer programs

The Technical Problem in a Nutshell 13

are able to handle that little bit of bookkeeping." So programmers have trained users, and then inadvertently been trapped by them into writing programs that accept six-digit dates.

Now, a computer programmer *can* write a piece of software that accepts six digit dates and interprets them correctly, even through the century change. However, it takes more effort to write software that does that. Any programmer on a tight schedule is going to be tempted to either (a) take a shortcut and just add the "19" on to the date, or (b) leave the six digit date as a six digit date, saving the year simply as "97." Because of this, many modern programs written for microcomputers—even in the late 1990's—have the exact same millenium bug hiding away in them.

One simple example of the millenium bug in a modern program is Borland's Paradox for Windows. I have this popular database program installed on the same computer I am using to write this book. It is a modern, 1990's program, written for Microsoft Windows. However, when you enter a date into a date field you get some very interesting behavior:

1) If you enter a date "7/15/97" the date is stored as "7/15/97". The two-digit year is kept as a two-digit year.

2) If you enter a date "7/15/1997" then the date is stored as "7/15/97". The 4-digit year is converted to a two-digit year. The program won't allow you to keep the 4-digit year.

3) If you enter a date "7/15/2000" then the date is stored as "7/15/2000". The 4-digit year is kept as a four-digit year.

4) If you enter a date "7/15/00" then the date is stored as "7/15/00". The 2-digit year is kept as a two-digit year. Someone was obviously thinking about the year 2000 problem when they coded this part of the Paradox program. However, their thinking was muddled. The program trains the user to use two digit dates for several years by stripping the "19" off of every year entered, and then requires a 4 digit date be entered in order to maintain year 2000 compatibility.

Many, many personal computer programs cause strange, quirky problems like this. A recent study[1] found that out of 4000 PC-based software packages, 2568 exhibited problematic behavior with the year 2000, and of these 2568, some 724 *claimed* to be year 2000 compliant. Even major, respected software developers like Microsoft and IBM are afraid to call their software "year 2000 compliant", instead opting for the phrase "year 2000 ready" begging the question, "ready for what?"

Lately, there has been a "quick test for year 2000 compatibility" floating around in computer circles. This "test" instructs you to set the system date on your computer to January 31, 1999, and the time to 11:57 PM, then turn off your computer for 5 minutes. Then you turn it back on to see if the system date has gone to 2000 correctly. The computer user is told that if he gets the year 2000, he doesn't have a problem. *That is horribly naïve.* It only explores one of a myriad of problems you might have. In short, the system date could go over to 2000 just fine, but if your database program, or your

---

[1] Douglas Hayward, "Beware Millenium Claims, Experts Warn", *TechWire*, May 29, 1997.

The Technical Problem in a Nutshell 15

accounting program, or whatever, thinks it is now the year 1900, you can still have plenty of trouble.

So what will happen when computers all around the world that have been programmed to recognize the year "00" as "1900" dutifully do exactly that? Misinterpretations of dates will abound, and all kinds of decisions will be made based on those misinterpretations. Some of those decisions will be petty, and easily rectified. Others could be life changing. Some could be world changing. And a lot of small, easily rectified decisions, all occurring at the same time could also be world changing.

The obvious solution to this problem is to fix the software that may misinterpret dates. From a purely technical, programmer's point of view, fixing any given date field in a program, or date entry routine is not a difficult problem. One need only go in and make a relatively minor modification to the software. It really shouldn't take a programmer more than a half an hour to fix a date entry routine, or five minutes to fix a date storage field.

Thinking in these terms tends to make the millenium bug appear relatively benign and easy to fix. *Many programmers fall into this trap when trying to assess the year 2000 problem.* However, there are a number of considerations that make the problem much more complex.

First of all, software consists of line after line of code that must all work together as a unit to produce a desired result. A program that works with six-digit dates will not usually work properly if a programmer merely changes the data areas where dates are stored to use eight-digit dates. The program itself must also be changed. For example, a part of a program that needs the full 4-digit year will generally interpret the two-digit year stored in memory by adding 1900 to whatever number is stored. So the program typically does a calculation like this:

$$97 + 1900 = 1997$$

in order to get the date "1997" to do further calculations. Now, if one just changed the two-digit year in memory into a four-digit year, but left this calculation in the program, it would then calculate the date as

$$1997 + 1900 = 3897$$

Not too nice.

Likewise, if the data entry routine that stores data in the new four-digit year isn't fixed, it will only collect two digits from the user, and it will still pass a two-digit value back to other parts of the program. So the computer operator will dutifully enter "97" when prompted, and the year "0097" will be stored in the four digit data, instead of 1997. Again, not too nice.

The bottom line is that even a single program can contain complexities that must *all* be ironed out in a logical, systematic way before the program will *consistently* handle dates correctly. If a program is not too big, and a programmer who is familiar with that program's code is handling the fixes, this is not a terrible problem. For example, a 5000 line accounting utility written in the c language can easily be straightened out in a day or so by the programmer who wrote it.

If the programmer making these changes is not familiar with the program, though, it can be a whole different matter. Once a few years have elapsed between when a programmer wrote a program and when he goes back to correct it, he will have forgotten what he did. If the program is huge (say 100,000+ lines), he will probably forget what he did. There's just too much information to

The Technical Problem in a Nutshell 17

remember. And worst of all, if that programmer didn't write the program to begin with, he's completely unfamiliar with it. It might take a new programmer a month to become familiar enough with a 5000 line accounting program that he should even dare to change it.

Given an unfamiliar program, a programmer has no way of knowing how that program deals with things like dates, *a priori*. He must sift through it with a fine toothed comb, and figure out what it does. In order to upgrade it and make it work right, he has to fix every spot where it handles dates in a consistent fashion. If he misses just one date handling routine, then somewhere or other that program is going to break and create erroneous data, or data that can be misinterpreted.

This is a very real problem that happens all the time in the software industry. I've even experienced it myself. Once I worked at a computer keyboard manufacturing company. One of my jobs was to maintain the firmware[2] for the keyboards, fixing bugs as they were reported. One day management was in a hurry to get a new software release out, and there was a small bug to be fixed. I was asked to forego the usual testing of all changes, which typically took several weeks. The bug could be fixed with a single byte of code, which seemed harmless enough, so I agreed. Little did I know, that one-byte change would create a major bug somewhere else in the code, resulting in the manufacture of 30,000 horribly defective keyboards. (The company went bankrupt about two months later.)

---

2 Firmware is software that is embedded in a microcontroller. All computer keyboards contain a microcontroller which detects keystrokes and sends keystroke information to the computer.

Of course, as soon as we start talking about fixing programs, we are assuming that you have the *source code* for that particular program in the first place. This source code is the original program, generally written in a computer language like Cobol, Pascal or C. It is what a software developer uses to make the program that you actually use on the computer, called the *executable*.[3] Generally, you only have the source code if you hired programmers who developed the software for you. (Provided you haven't lost it.) Software companies have, for decades, been in the practice of developing programs and then selling the executables while keeping the source code as a closely guarded secret. So most of the software that businesses run on their computers is executable only. *They have no source code, and no ability to change the program if it needs date fixes.*

If you don't have the source code to a program, then you are completely dependent on whoever does to get your date problems fixed. For example, I don't have the source code to Borland's Paradox. There is absolutely nothing I can do to fix the date problem it has. I can only

a) Use the program and hope that it's date problem won't affect me when the new millenium hits,

b) Stop using the program, and find another one that works right, or,

c) Hope that the manufacturer will upgrade the product and fix the date problem before the millenium turns over.

---

3 The executable is made by running a *compiler*—another program—on the source code.

The Technical Problem in a Nutshell 19

In short, I am at the mercy of the software developer. In the end Borland decided to do something even worse than I imagined. They sold their Paradox product to another software manufacturer. Now, I've bought that manufacturer's products before, and they've been full of bugs—bugs enough that I've had to stop using them and buy something else. So I don't want to buy a product that's made by them. I don't trust their programmers to be thorough and accurate, and I fully expect them to sell me something that will cause more problems than it solves.

I suppose Borland could have done worse. They could have simply gone out of business, like so many software developers have over the years. Or they could have sold their Paradox code to a competitor who subsequently shelved it, or quietly incorporated parts of it into their own product.

So the millenium bug is compounded by the complexity of most software, along with the fact that millions and millions of people as well as companies have no power whatsoever to simply fix the bug. They are dependent upon software developers, some of whom have gone out of business, some of whom have merged with others and can no longer be located, and some of whom are just downright incompetent to make the needed changes in a timely, accurate fashion. Even those who are competent may decide to take advantage of a bad situation and charge an arm and a leg for an upgrade.

This is the technical side of the millenium bug in a nutshell.

3. Will the Technical Problem Crash the World?

It is truly hard to tell if the technical side of the millenium bug will crash all the world's computers and bring civilization as we know it to a grinding halt. The repercussions of the millenium bug contain a high degree of uncertainty. It isn't like a comet headed straight toward the earth, where the trajectories could be computed with great precision. The complexities of the world's computer networks are too confusing to make such certain predictions.

More than a few people in positions of power seem to think that the millenium bug could spell disaster. For example, Emmett Paige, Jr., Assistant Secretary of Defense said that "the consequences might be catastrophic."[1] The Office of Management and Budget of the US government has stated that "the potential impact on Federal programs if this problem is not corrected is substantial, and potentially very serious."[2] Joel C.

---

1 Statement by the Honorable Emmett Paige, Jr., Assistant Secretary of Defense, before the Committee on Government Reform and Oversight, Subcommittee on Government Management, Information and Technology, US House of Representatives, April 16, 1996.

Will the Technical Problem Crash the World? 21

Willemssen of the Government Accounting Office states that "if systems that millions of Americans have come to rely on for regular benefits malfunction, the ensuing delays could be disastrous."[3] Retired Air Force General Thomas McInerney, in assessing the potential military problem, even went so far as to say "I think the president or vice president should declare that this is a potential national emergency."[4]

Last year, Senator Daniel Patrick Moynihan sent President Clinton a public letter advising him that the millenium bug was "a problem which could have extreme negative economic consequences." Moynihan asserted that the economy could be "facing chaos" and suggested the possibility that the military should "take command of dealing with the problem." Moynihan summed up his letter by stating that "The computer has been a blessing; if we don't act quickly, however, it could become the curse of the age."[5]

These are not cracker-jack self-appointed experts with a new twist to sell the public some kind of doom-and-gloom scenario. They are men with serious responsibilities and serious concerns. Of course, you can find

---

2 *Getting Federal Computers Ready for 2000*, Report of the US Office of Management and Budget, February 6, 1997.
3 Statement by Joel C. Willemssen, Director of Information Resources Management, GAO Accounting and Information Management Division, before the Committee on Government Reform and Oversight, Subcommittee on Government Management, Information and Technology, US House of Representatives, April, 1996.
4 "Year 2000 may ambush US military", *Computer World*, January 2, 1997.
5 Available at the internet site http://www.comlinks.com/gov/moyn0731.htm.

experts of one bent or another out there who promise to help you survive the trouble ahead. And people will call them crackpots and question their motives. For example, Gary North has taken a lot of heat for sending out fliers by the millions advising prospective subscribers that "A bank run like no other will hit every major bank on earth in 1999. A worldwide panic is now inevitable. It has literally been programmed into bank's computers. Everything you own is now at stake. But there are steps you can take now that will give you a head start on this crisis . . . ."[6] Certainly his motives could be questioned. Even major magazine articles have spread the scare. *Newsweek* Magazine recently ran a cover story "The Day the World Shuts Down" featuring a picture of giant broken computers and smoke flying at a crowd of yuppies running away in stark terror.[7] Maybe they are just trying to sell magazines.

It is easy to get cynical about all of these frightening scenarios, especially if you have a background in programming. After all, people often do have ulterior motives for saying what they say. The newsletter writer's motives may seem dubious. He wants to sell subscriptions, and inspiring fear *is* a great way to do it. Perhaps *Newsweek* wants to sell magazines, too.[8] Does Senator Moynihan have an agenda, too? Would he like to take

---

6 At the time of this writing you could request a free copy of this report from North's web site, http://www.garynorth.com, a site well worth investigating.
7 *Newsweek*, June 2, 1997, p. 52.
8 For that matter, you might wonder whether I'm just trying to make money writing this book. I should like to think not, but then if I didn't, I doubt I could justify taking the time to write it.

Will the Technical Problem Crash the World? 23

credit for being the man who saved the government? Do the officials from alphabet-soup government agencies want to get higher-ups to move, or to give their MIS departments more funding? And then what of the calm assessments that everything is under control, and there is nothing to worry about? Are these statements just coming from people who don't want to admit they have a crisis?

Are people just blowing hot air? Or should the possibilities they describe be taken seriously? Well, there is one thing to be said: *if governments and big companies are putting money and manpower into the problem, then they are taking it seriously.* Real effort is a very good measure of seriousness.

A recent survey of large US companies by the Society for Information Management found that nearly 30% of total information technology spending over the next three years would go to year 2000 conversion projects.[9] This suggests that business is taking the problem *very* seriously. A few companies have made actual numbers public. For example, Allstate Insurance Co. is spending some $40 million on its millenium bugs. Mars, the candy bar company, is spending $100 million.[10] Merril Lynch is spending $200 million.[11] Citibank is spending $200 million. Union Pacific Railroad started fixing its bugs in 1995, and is planning to put 200,000 man-hours into the fix. Meanwhile, initial estimates of $2.3 billion to fix all federal computer systems[12] have—only six months

---

9 "And now for the bad news", Bob Violino and Bruce Caldwell, *Information Week*, April 21, 1997.
10 *Op. Cit.*, Moynihan letter.
11 *Newsweek*, June 2, 1997, p. 57.
12 *Getting Federal Computers Ready for 2000,* Report of the US

later—been adjusted to $3.8 billion.[13] As agencies get deeper into the problem, they are realizing that its magnitude is larger than first believed. For example, the IRS asked Congress for $342 billion in July 1997 to fix its millenium bugs, up from its $84 billion request in the Clinton fiscal year 1998 budget.[14] This increased to $684 billion in September.[15] State and local governments are also planning to spend large sums to fix the problem. For example, Los Angeles County estimates $30 million in conversion costs. The State of Nebraska estimates $28 million; North Carolina estimates $300 million, and has invoked emergency rules to short-circuit the normal bidding process on government contracts so that they can get moving on the fix.[16]

In short, at least some governments, government agencies, and businesses really are taking this problem seriously. There is no doubt. They are putting money and manpower behind it.

However, not everyone is taking the millenium bug as seriously as they ought. For example, although the Social Security Administration began work on the problem in 1989, the Department of Energy didn't even begin to address the issue until a week *after* it received a House subcommittee request for a status report in April, 1996.[17]

Office of Management and Budget, February 6, 1997, p. 4.
13 "IRS Y2K Woes Cost More", Sharon Machlis, *Computerworld*, September 15, 1997.
14 *Federal Computer Week*, June 23, 1997.
15 *Computerworld*, September 15, 1997.
16 John Wagner, "Two-digit computer chaos looming", *The News Observer*, April 6, 1997.
17 Statement by Representative Stephen Horn, Subcommittee on Government Management, Information and Technology, July

Will the Technical Problem Crash the World? 25

The Gartner Group likewise predicts that fewer than 25% of state and local government computer systems will be ready for the year 2000 in time. In a July 10, 1997 article in the *Washington Times*, it was pointed out that the Office of Management and Budget report issued on that date said only 6% of federal computers have been fixed so far. 35% of the computers involved have not even been analyzed to see what will need to be fixed. The *Post* article pits private analysts' assessments of "not on a time schedule that looks like it's going to be doable" and "way behind the eight ball" with government statements of "I think we're on track."[18]

A few surveys have been done in the business sector to determine levels of awareness. The results have not been encouraging. For example, in a survey of 150 large companies, mostly Fortune 500, only 13% have *implemented a plan* to correct the issue and 18% have *developed a plan*. That leaves some 69% in limbo.[19] The Japanese Information Service Industry Association reported that about 28% of Japanese industry and only about 13% of Japanese government organizations had begun repairs as of mid-1996. Likewise, in the UK, as of May, 1997, 90% of bigger companies had yet to even complete an internal audit or assessment of the year 2000 problem they faced.[20] Again, a survey of 697 European

---

30, 1996.
18 Rajiv Chandrasekaran, "Government Said to Move Too Slowly on Year 2000 Computer Problem", *The Washington Post*, July 10, 1997, p. E1.
19 Randal Mikkelsen, "Year 2000 computer problem seen striking early", Reuters, June 20, 1997.
20 Neil Winton, "Smaller UK Companies Face Millenium Bug Sting", Reuters, May 13, 1997.

companies reported that two thirds have no budget for repairs, and only 56% think it is a serious problem.[21]

Such statistics are not reassuring.

Add to this the simple fact that maybe 80% of all ordinary software projects are brought in late, and the fact that testing year 2000 fixes can become practically impossible. Mainframes that lack the capacity to run new programs while keeping up with the data flow required by the old programs cannot test the fixes. Neither can computer networks that are interacting with the real world and with other computers that are not year-2000 compliant.

Anyone with programming experience can tell you that testing a program and debugging it can be the most painful, time-consuming and unpredictable part of the development process. Yet many companies and government agencies are leaving themselves no room for problems by planning to complete their fixes in November or December 1999. No wonder the GAO's David Willemssen testified before Congress[22] that

> "OMB's perspective that agencies have made a good start and that no mission-critical systems were reported to be behind schedule would seem to imply that there is no cause for alarm. On the contrary, we believe ample evidence exists that OMB and key federal agencies need to heighten their levels of concern and move with more urgency."

To date no big company, no government organization, anywhere in the world, has announced that they

---

21 Techwire, April 21, 1997.
22 David Willemssen, Testimony before Congress, July 10, 1997.

Will the Technical Problem Crash the World?   27

have successfully completed their year 2000 conversions. Not one.

Given the bare facts, we have to conclude that the millenium bug is a serious problem. Large organizations are getting worried about it—worried enough to pour millions of dollars into fixing it, rather than into revenue-producing projects. Likewise, we have to conclude that a significant percentage of large organizations *are* going to plunge into the year 2000 without fixes in place or without *tested* fixes in place. That is a simple consequence of the significant percentage of organizations that either aren't dealing with the problem, or are leaving themselves no margin for error.

In short, *something* is going to happen. We can't tell what—but *something will happen.* The programs that people, companies and governments depend on will not all get fixed in time, and they will be running in January, 2000. We have crossed the line beyond which a complete fix is even possible.

4. Doomsday at the Doorstep

There is some value in looking at a few typical doomsday scenarios, just to imagine what could happen come January, 2000. Such scenarios should be taken with a grain of salt. One should not underestimate people's resourcefulness in times of trouble, and one should not underestimate the ability of large organizations to continue in existence even when common sense dictates that they will not. Both you and I have worked at companies that have been horribly managed, and justly deserved to disappear from the face of the earth, and yet they seem to survive and carry on somehow or other.

The real value of looking at these scenarios is to understand the kinds of possibilities that are going to be paraded before the public eye with increasing frequency as the year 2000 approaches. And at bottom, they *could* happen. Some computers *are* going to break in 2000. That much is a foregone conclusion, and the extent of the problem this breakdown will create is largely unpredictable. The possibilities are simply endless. Even Gary North, who is advising his subscribers to move to the country and plan for serious survivalist-style scenarios may not be so far off base when the calendar actually does turn.

Doomsday Scenario #1: A Failing Business

Any business is dependent on a variety of organizations and people to stay in business. For example, it is dependent on a number of suppliers to provide crucial raw materials and services. It is dependent upon customers to buy products and to order products. It is dependent upon employees to provide labor to develop and fabricate products, sell products and service customer accounts. Likewise, a business is dependent on other organizations to sell its products, including newspapers, printers, magazines and electronic media as well as telephone systems and even the internet. Then the business is dependent on various service-oriented businesses like banks and builders or real estate investors (to rent property), shippers to deliver products and supplies, and so on.

Each of these dependencies could be viewed as a vulnerability to the millenium bug. If suppliers couldn't supply raw materials, if customers couldn't pay their bills on time, if employees couldn't collect their paychecks, or if key sales outlets went away, a business could be seriously hurt if not entirely driven out of business.

Considering that only *some* businesses are dealing with the millenium bug, it is completely reasonable to assume that many if not most businesses will find that some organizations it depends on will not be dependable at the turn of the millenium. Even if we assume that 90% of all businesses will be year 2000 compliant come January 1, 2000 (and given the statistics we have already reviewed, that would appear to be a very optimistic number) then 10% *won't be*. Suppose that of the 10% that aren't, 10% face major problems. Then 1% of all businesses will be facing major problems with their computer systems. That is still a *huge* number, and something that no business dare ignore. Even a very small company can probably find a hundred organizations that it depends on in one way or another, which suggests that every company is going to face glitches in the year 2000, even if they have completely dealt with their own millenium bugs. And some businesses could find themselves in a position where they are facing more than just a glitch.

Obviously there are many, many different ways things could go wrong to damage a business. The business could fail because it can no longer manufacture and deliver its product due to internal millenium bugs. Or a key supplier could fail, or that business' bank could fail or . . . .

Let's consider just one possibility in detail: Suppose that customers cannot pay for products on time because either their internal computers have fouled up or the payment systems aren't working, or because the business under discussion can't bill because its own computers are fouled up. Then again, perhaps customers can't pay because they're having cash flow problems because their customers can't pay them.

Any of these possibilities is real. Billing and payment systems normally depend upon time dependent information. Typical terms of sale in business are *net 30 days*, which means that a business orders a product, and then pays for it in 30 days. Most businesses string out paying their bills until the last possible minute to improve their cash flow (e.g. the amount of money they have in the bank). So a bill dated September 15 on net 30 terms gets paid *on* October 15, and not a minute before. The problem is, when a bill dated December 15, 1999 gets saved in a computer as 12-15-99, it won't get paid until 1-15-

Doomsday at the Doorstep

100, but the computer won't ever reach year 100. It will roll over to year 00 instead, and the bill won't get paid at all.

Now, when the biller doesn't get paid, he will issue a past due notice of some sort, and hope to get paid soon. If he still doesn't get paid, he may send more notices, make a phone call, or send the account to collections. A company that is having year 2000 problems may not be able to pay its bills, or even figure out what those bills are until it gets its computer problems straightened out.

So, the business that shipped a product and doesn't get paid on time will have cash flow trouble. Typically a business plans on financing its customers with net 30 terms. A certain amount of capital is always tied up in this financing. If customers can't pay for 3 or 6 months for any reason, then the supplier is forced to multiply the amount of money tied up financing customers by 3 or 6 times, respectively. This can amount to tying up a huge amount of money very suddenly—money that needs to be used to meet payroll, to pay suppliers, advertising bills, etc. Employees aren't going to accept an I.O.U. from one of their employer's customers instead of a check at the end of the week. In short, a business can get strapped for cash when its customers don't pay their bills on time, and the results can be disastrous.

The business faced with cash flow problems can normally attempt to obtain a loan, possibly using its customer's debts (receivables) or some other asset as collateral. However, obtaining such a loan may be difficult or very costly when the millenium bug strikes. If large numbers of businesses are hit with similar problems at the same time, they will bid up the price of such loans, and bankers will raise the requirements for such loans to the point that many businesses will not even qualify. The banks may even go out of business themselves.

Most vulnerable will be businesses that are marginal to begin with. If a business is already obtaining loans on its receivables, or if it is already having cash flow problems, adding more to it could easily drive that business into bankruptcy. Even otherwise healthy businesses could fail if the millenium bug proves sufficiently disruptive.

Once bankruptcies reach a certain level, they can snowball because otherwise healthy businesses have to absorb the cost of the bankruptcies. In other words, if a key customer can't pay his bills, he may not be meeting payroll either. His suppliers may be cutting him off. Or his customers may be going bankrupt. In the end, that customer may not just fail to pay its bills for 90 days. That customer may go bankrupt as a result of what it is facing. Then its bills will never get paid, and it will no longer be a source of income.

In such a way, a business could be driven into bankruptcy itself.

Doomsday Scenario #2: Revolution

Taking a step up in scale, one can ponder what might happen if one of any of a myriad of government payments don't come through. Whether it be Social Security, Medicare, food stamps, unemployment, welfare, or paychecks to government employees, many, many people are dependent on government money. What would happen if these government payments simply *stopped*, be it for a month, six months, or even permanently?

Any number of year 2000 software glitches could stop these government payments from coming. The computers that issue the checks could foul up, and stop issuing checks to people they think have yet to be born.

Doomsday at the Doorstep 33

The data entry routines may not allow new people to be entered into the system. Then again, the computers that maintain account balances for the various agencies might stop running. Or what if the government fails to pay the interest on the national debt, or ceases to redeem government debt? The debt-based funding which is paying the government's way could dry up instantly, and government money would stop flowing. Again, what if people thought (or knew) that the IRS couldn't collect taxes because it was mired down in computer problems? What if they just stopped volunteering to pay their taxes?

All of these possibilities are potential glitches that could stop government payments from coming. Some of them are very real possibilities. Although social security may not stop (since the Social Security Administration has been working on fixing its year 2000 problems since 1989), the Department of Agriculture (who runs the food stamp program) is, at the time of this writing, in the worst position of all federal agencies with respect to its year 2000 fixes. They haven't even finished *evaluating* their computer systems, let alone started to reprogram them.[1]

Now, what will happen when those government payments don't arrive?

At one level, we can expect total gridlock. The Social Security Administration, for example, delivers some 50 million payments per month. If one percent of these had a problem, it would generate a half-million phone calls to Social Security offices. There is simply no way that a few hundred Social Security offices could handle that

---

1 "Government Said to Move Too Slowly on Year 2000 Computer Problem", Rajiv Chandrasekaran, *Washington Post*, July 10, 1997, p. E01.

kind of telephone volume. The result would be *total* gridlock. Most people would never get through to find out where their money was or why it was the wrong amount. The same could be said of just about any welfare-oriented government office. Yet one would have to assume that unless that office knew you had a problem, it would not be able to correct it, so getting through would be imperative in order to get your payment, or get it corrected. The result could be absolute chaos.

Given a lockout, many people simply would not be able to make ends meet. They couldn't live. They lack the skills, the strength, and often the inclination to survive on their own, especially on a moment's notice. Although America's senior citizens might express their displeasure at the ballot box, many other groups will not be so polite. Will those who live on food stamps think they have a right to food at no cost, and start looting grocery stores? Will those who depend on government checks to pay their rent think they have a right to a house and shoot the landlord when he comes to collect the rent?

Isolated incidents could turn into riots in areas with a high concentration of people dependent on government payouts. Such civil unrest could be like lighting a match in a dynamite factory. Racial and ethnic relations are stressed in the United States, to say the least. A number of authors have already outlined the shape of a racial civil war which is brewing up in the US.[2,3] If riots in some area simply could not be quelled, perhaps because too many people were rioting, perhaps because police de-

---

2   Thomas W. Chittum, *Civil War Two* (American Eagle Publications:1997).
3   Carl Rowan, *The Coming Race War in America* (Little Brown and Co.:1996).

partments were disabled due to their own year 2000 problems, those riots could escalate into an out-and-out civil war which could dissolve the government as we know it.

In short, although the millenium bug could not overthrow a nation populated by patient, loving people who are willing to care for each other and pull together in times of difficulty, it certainly could push a people rife with mistrust, hatred and selfishness into the abyss of civil war and revolution.

Doomsday Scenario #3: Foreign Invasion

A military organization must be able to deliver men and equipment where they are needed in a timely manner. Likewise, they must be able to detect enemy movements and intrusions. Various units must be able to communicate with each other, etc. Any military that cannot carry out these basic functions is vulnerable to attack.

The armies of most western countries are highly dependent upon computers—computers that may not function properly in the year 2000 unless fixed. On the other hand, less technologically advanced nations, such as China, are not nearly so dependent on computers, and therefore not as vulnerable to the millenium bug.

Now, an enemy could interpret even the possibility of computer failure as an invitation to attack at the moment the clock turns over. Then, if the possibility turns to reality, and some country's military might is hobbled, be it for a few weeks or a few months, an enemy might be passing by a golden opportunity to strike.

Some businesses that are taking the millenium bug seriously clearly see it as a potential advantage in the marketplace around the turn of the millenium. Banks, for example, that are year 2000 compliant should be able to attract customers away from banks that are fumbling around with the bug.[4] *We have to view national interests in the same light.* A nation that prepares for the millenium changeover diligently, and makes sure its own military will not suffer computer glitches will have a competitive advantage over a country that does not prepare. With a world full of animosities, it would be naive to think that no one would try to exploit such weaknesses, even if only to scare their enemies.

Perhaps it is not nice to contemplate an unprovoked invasion, but some countries have no scruples about such things. Worse, millenium bug breakdowns might provide an excuse of provocation. For example, if a nation defaulted on paying the interest on its national debt as a result of the millenium bug, someone to whom that nation was indebted might take it as provocation, while others holding the defaulted debt may be happy to sit on the sidelines and watch.

A good example of such a scenario might be a Chinese invasion of Taiwan. Both the Taiwanese and the US military are much more dependent on computers than China. China is buying up US debt faster than any other country on the face of the globe, and they haven't shied from threatening the US with nuclear attack, from buying up US technology and military secrets, and bribing pub-

---

[4] For example, when the Bank of Boston's David Iacino testified before Congress, he plainly stated "The millenium prepared financial institution will enjoy a competitive advantage over other banks' inaciton. Cross selling of additional products and services to a nervous customer base will provide an opportunity for additional fee income to the millenium compliant bank." (July 10, 1997 testimony).

Doomsday at the Doorstep

lic officials all within the past year. Likewise they have successfully obtained tribute from the US in the form of "most favored nation" trade status. If the US had problems with its debt obligations, China could conceivably dump that debt on the market and take Taiwan as repayment, while using military disabilities to ensure a quick and certain victory. Worse, a quick victory might inspire more ambitious plans. Could China turn an eye toward Japan, while North Korea gobbles up South Korea. Perhaps Saddam Hussein will wake up and decide to try for Kuwait again, and God knows what else.

Now, as I said, these doomsday scenarios should be taken with a grain of salt. We don't really know what will happen. One would hope that someone would have the sense to make sure that mission-critical military systems, etc., would get fixed in time. Regardless, what we can count on is that these kind of scenarios are going to be laid out before the public's eyes again and again and again in the next couple years. The June 2, 1997 *Newsweek* article was nothing less than a litany of scary possibilities. It is just the beginning. *And that is certain to have serious consequences.*

5. The Great Media Scare

March 5, 1992: I hang up the phone. The second it hits the cradle, it begins to ring again. I knew it would. I answer it and patiently lead another terrified person through the routine to check for the Michelangelo virus:

"Are you at your computer now?"
"Yes"
"Okay, then type C-H-K-D-S-K at the command prompt and press 'Enter'."
"Okay, it's running."
"Tell me when it's done."
". . . . Done"
"At the bottom of the report that CHKDSK displays on the screen it tells you the 'total bytes memory'. What number did it report?"
"All right . . . 655,360 total bytes memory."
"Good, that means you don't have the virus."
"Oh, thank you so much!"

So it would continue all day long, until I got up and went home, the phone still ringing nervously. I knew that tomorrow, if anyone had been infected, I'd only be able to offer them an "I'm sorry."

Michelangelo was discovered in mid-1991 and added to an ever-growing list of potentially dangerous viruses, but few people thought it was especially dangerous at the

The Great Media Scare

time. Then, in December 1992, the computer manufacturer Leading Edge shipped about 500 computers that were infected with the virus. A customer detected it, and Leading Edge made this fact public on January 28, 1992. This was the beginning of the Michelangelo scare, barely a month before the date the virus was set to detonate. A day later UPI wrote up the story, giving the virus magical powers to replicate, and calling it the "third most common", representing 14% of all virus infection reports, some 6000 infections reported at the time. By February 11, the infection had blossomed into something that affected "millions of personal computers around the world." By mid-February, anti-virus software vendors were throwing around figures on the order of 5 million infections, and the press was gobbling them up. By the first of March, worldwide public reaction could only be described as hysterical. Infection rates of 25% to 35% of all computers were being quoted. Stores carrying anti-virus software were mobbed and sold out. Newspapers were trying to brace people for the worst with headlines like "The Mass Murderer Will Attack On Friday", "Thousands Of PCs Could Crash Friday", "Deadly Virus Set To Wreak Havoc Tomorrow", "Paint It Scary." Popular television programs like *Nightline* were telling viewers that the virus was "the equivalent of doing germ warfare in your own neighborhood" while giving viewers insane methods for dealing with the virus, like leaving one's computer on the whole of March 5 through March 7. By the morning of March 6, everyone realized that the Michelangelo scare was a big dud.[1]

---

1 For a good account of the Michelangelo scare, read George Smith's *The Virus Creation Labs* (American Eagle

Analyzing Michelangelo and the Year 2000

In order to understand what is likely to happen with the millenium bug, it is important to understand the dynamics of the Michelangelo scare, both in its similarities to the millenium bug, and its differences.

Both the Michelangelo virus and the millenium bug are products of technology gone awry—technology that the average person doesn't really begin to understand, and technology that the average journalist doesn't understand. Very few people know how a virus works. And I don't think *anybody* understands how the millenium bug is going to work in the world's computer networks, even though on the level of one line of code it is simple enough.

Both Michelangelo and the millenium bug offer the specter of widespread high-tech destruction that will strike on a specific date that everybody knows in advance.

These two factors, a basic ignorance on the part of the general public that is not easily remedied, and the possibility of high-tech destruction, make for a first class news story. People will eat it up. The fact that a reporter cannot easily analyze the danger from a technical viewpoint means journalists have to rely on "experts" to tell them what is going on in both situations.

Where Michelangelo and the millenium bug differ is that the millenium bug makes Michelangelo look like a Sunday afternoon picnic. The great error reporters made when trying to fathom what would happen when

---

Publications:1994).

Michelangelo went off is that they trusted one or two vocal people in the anti-virus industry who stood to profit heavily from a scare.[2] Only belatedly did they realize that not everyone who dealt with viruses saw things in the same light. Some virus experts were expecting perhaps 10,000 hits by the virus. They didn't catch on to the fact that for many companies, government agencies, etc., it was business as usual both before the fateful day and when it hit.

The millenium bug differs from Michelangelo in this one crucial point. Big businesses and government are spending huge amounts of money and man-hours to fix the bug, and they're doing it quite apart from the prompting of the press. Plenty of people may have spent money on anti-virus products during the first part of 1992, but they were doing it because the press had scared them. Today, the problems that may result from the millenium bug are only dawning on the press. Yet large organizations have been working on the problem for years. In other words real people—the programmers, managers and businessmen out there in the trenches—know that the millenium bug is a real problem and they know they have real work to do to fix it.

How a Scare Starts

Michelangelo had been known for some time before anybody really took notice of it. Then, almost overnight,

---

2   And incidently, they did profit greatly. John McAfee, for example, who was quoted again and again warning of "millions" of hits was able to take his anti-virus company, McAfee Associates, public and pocket a cool $7 million a few months later.

it went from being just another virus to the pariah of the world. The event that catalyzed this transformation was the Leading Edge announcement that it had shipped 500 computers with the virus on it. Leading Edge made that fact public for the sake of damage control. They didn't want their customers to lose all their data on March 6, and end up getting blamed for it. In 1992, mass distribution of a virus by a major manufacturer was a newsworthy event. Furthermore, reporting it was a public service. From there, the story of the virus took off.

The dynamics of the Michelangelo scare aren't all that surprising, when you think about it. A journalist who isn't a technical whiz must approach a story by first going to the so-called experts. He must talk to them. If he can, he'll find a few and compare their opinions and ideas. However, he is operating from a position of ignorance. If the expert tells him the sky is falling, what business does he have contradicting him? If *all* the experts he talks to agree that the sky is falling, then he will naturally be convinced that it really is.

In 1992 the most renowned anti-virus expert in the United States, if not the world, was John McAfee. His shareware SCAN program was known everywhere. So it was only natural that he would be the first person a journalist would look to for an opinion. His opinion that this was a very big problem set the wheels in motion for the media blitz that occurred.

The second element that made Michelangelo so big was the simple fact that the story had all the right elements to sell big. And the more it was told, the bigger it sold. The bottom line in any media operation is to publish stories that sell. Sales are what count because sales are what make a media-oriented business profitable.

For print media, like newspapers, sales have two dimensions: First, it means readers who will buy the

The Great Media Scare 43

newspaper, either on the newsstand or through a subscription. Second, it means advertisers who buy advertising space in the newspapers.

For radio and television, viewers do not generate revenue directly for the station. However, advertising rates are determined by the number of people who watch a program. The more people who watch, the higher that program's rating will be, and the higher the rating, the more an advertising slot on that program will bring.

In either case, a media outlet must cater to its advertisers and to its target audience, the financial goal being to reach the largest audience without offending advertisers. This applies to almost any kind of media. Whether it is a general city newspaper that tries to attract readers ranging from a shaved and pierced lesbian tattoo artist to the commanding general at the local army base, or whether it is a national newspaper that targets conservative, middle class Christians, the same basic rules apply. The target audience may vary considerably. The products advertised may vary considerably. In any event, the media outlet still seeks to reach the largest audience without offending advertisers.

From this point of view, a computer scare is perfect. Michelangelo was an enemy that *everybody* could hate, an enemy who could hurt almost *anybody*. Reporting on this enemy would offend nobody, help everybody, and keep readers and listeners coming back for more until the day of doom arrived.

Now, let's take a look at the millenium bug, and its potential to cause a scare. Certainly, it has all the right elements for a scare. It is even more ominous than Michelangelo. It is a product of the technological age, and not easily understood. It has a fixed day on which doom could potentially rain down on us. There are plenty of experts who are really worried about it, and their ranks are swelling. Big companies are spending lots of money on it. Many of the things that were manufactured by the media for Michelangelo—hype—don't need to be manufactured for the millenium bug. The media need not magnify the voice of one expert like it was the voice of God. Plenty of experts agree that the bug is a problem. They don't need to run stories about how the "virus has invaded Capitol Hill"[3] to scare congressional staffs. Capitol Hill, in this case, is spending billions on the problem and holding hearings on it. They're well aware of the danger, and getting more and more nervous.

Right now, the time isn't right for a big scare. The bug won't detonate for two years, and the average person will only focus on something like this for a month. Then the public gets tired of it and wants to have their ears tickled with something new. Besides, someone thinking about it casually will be hard to convince that it can't be fixed in time.

Another element that is lacking is a major event connected with the millenium bug to set things off. The time isn't ripe for such an event quite yet, but as the day of reckoning draws nearer, that event is almost guaranteed to come. There are a number of possibilities for what this major event might be. One possibility is that programs which depend on dates in the future could run into glitches due to the millenium bug. This could cause a major problem for some company or bank or what have you that involves the general public. It might involve a state or federal government, which switches over to fiscal year 2000 between July 1 and October 1, 1999. Generally, when such glitches develop, they are kept

---

[3] AP Newswire, March 3, 1992.

quiet if they cause merely internal problems. Once the public is involved, though, they cannot be kept quiet.

These glitches will most likely show up when programs that look into the future malfunction in some way. That is how the Social Security Administration came to realize it had a problem: programs that were looking ten years into the future didn't work right. In another instance, a few prisoners who were supposed to be released in the 21st century have received surprise pardons from a computer that thought they were supposed to be freed in the early 20th century. A 104-year-old Kansas woman was sent a notice to enter Kindergarten.[4] So it may be only a matter of time before something happens that will focus national media attention.

Then again, rather than a technical problem that focuses public attention, it may be something administrative or legislative. For example, bankers are considering a bank holiday on December 31, 1999 to give banks an extra day of testing. The mere suggestion of such a possibility seems to have stirred things up a bit. Or David Iacino of the Bank of Boston has been lobbying Congress for a law to excuse banks from liability as a result of the bug.[5] Passage of such a law could focus public attention.

Another possibility is that, as the day of reckoning draws near, the growing realization that the millenium bug is not going to be fixed in time will cause leaders to make statements that will gain public notice. For example, some government agency head will go public with the fact that it cannot fix its bugs in time given current funding, and outline a doomsday scenario that will take

---

4 *Newsweek*, June 2, 1997, p.56.
5 *American Banker*, February 18, 1998.

place. Of course, this would be a maneuver on the part of that agency to get more funding. However, it could be the event that catalyzes a panic. Again, perhaps some major company will have its credit rating lowered and watch its stock drop through the floor because it isn't dealing with the millenium bug. Lots of things could happen as the time to fix the bug ebbs away and inaction turns to realization and then to panic.

The Newsweek Article

The June 2, 1997 cover story "The Day the World Crashes" in *Newsweek* is an excellent preview of how the media is going to react. The article isn't saying doomsday is here quite yet. However, it paints a picture of almost certain trouble and possible devastation. Authors Levy and Hafner avoid predicting major problems themselves, as is proper and fitting for reporters for a major news magazine. Instead, they review a myriad of possible scenarios, while letting the experts they quote do the disaster-predicting. The authors' own predictions are limited to mild and temporary dislocations. However, they do go so far as to advise readers that "It may be best to keep a few dollars under the mattress" in case of banking problems and to "Stock up on candles and flashlight batteries" in case the power goes out.[6]

In a way, the *Newsweek* article is almost schizophrenic. It's recommended actions for dealing with the problem are almost a joke in the light of the potential dangers they discuss. After all, stocking up on candles hardly seems like appropriate preparedness if there is even a 1 in 1000 chance that the nuclear reactor 20 miles

---

6 *Newsweek*, June 2, 1997, p. 57.

away from your home is going to blow at midnight. However, *Newsweek* is not *The National Enquirer*. It is not a magazine that is normally given to sensationalism or alarmism. The mainstream media isn't going to report stories that will convince you to turn off the tube or cancel your subscription and head for the hills. It's just not in their interests to do that. To find such a mainstream magazine advocating *any* kind of survivalist-style preparations in case of bank closings and power outages is *very* unusual—even if those preparations seem woefully inadequate in the face of the potential danger.

The Next Two Years

Newsweek's story is just the tip of the iceberg. As the world and the media wake up to the reality of the millenium bug, more and more stories like Newsweek's are going to find their way into the hands of alarmed readers. In the six months since the first edition of this book came out, media attention to the problem has grown exponentially, and the tone of the articles has betrayed a growing sense of alarm.

Obviously it is very difficult to predict exactly what the media is going to do two years in the future, especially in a culture that has become expert in denying basic reality. However, it would appear that the temptation to make the most of the millenium bug could easily become almost irresistible for the media as the day of reckoning draws near.

Consider that the tone of stories could undergo a dramatic change come January 1, 1999. That's because the federal government, along with a fair number of millenium bug experts, are recommending programming changes be completed by then to allow a full year for testing. This is a major deadline. If the changes aren't completed by then, stories could change in tone quickly from "will we make it?" to "we're not going to make it."

The reader of this book should keep an eye on the media's growing response to the millenium bug. That's the only way to anticipate an all-out scare. Watch for an increasing frequency of stories about the problem. Consider the tone of the stories. Are they merely wondering if the problem will be fixed on time, or are they asserting that it won't? Watch for stories about real problems already occurring as a result of the millenium bug.

When the frequency and urgency of these stories starts to pick up, you can expect them to snowball into all-out panic. The more the public hears about the problem, the more fearsome it becomes, and the more fearsome it becomes, the more the public wants to hear.

Next, you should look at what various authors are recommending to their readers. When *Newsweek* tells people to stuff a little cash in the mattress and stock up on candles and flashlight batteries, one has to assume that at least some people will take such a recommendation seriously and do it (provided they can remember two and a half years later). Others will take the recommendation seriously, and then start to reason it out a little more. They'll realize that their refrigerator and electric stove won't work either if the power goes out, so they'll buy a camping stove, some propane bottles and canned food. And so on.

You have to realize that most people won't take any action to protect themselves the first time they hear about a potential problem. It's common knowledge in mail order that the average person has to see a product advertised or mentioned at least seven times before he will buy. The same could be said of warnings about the millenium bug. The first warning will spur a few to action. However, as warnings and recommendations multiply, people will begin to take them seriously and act on them. Once sufficient attention is focused on the millenium bug, people will run for cover, just like they did during the Michelangelo scare. Only this time, they won't be running to stores to buy anti-virus programs or calling up virus experts. They'll be taking their money out of the bank. They'll be planning for hard-core survivalist scenarios (or they'll be planning to loot and pillage in a time of chaos).

Mind you, this is not some doom-and-gloom scenario. The mainstream press is *already* starting to recommend such actions!

Censorship and the Underground Media

One final factor bears consideration even though it is very unlikely: censorship. Will the press—for one reason or another—censor what's going on with the millenium bug, or misinform the public about the general state of readiness for it?

It is becoming a well known fact that the mainstream press in America today often censors news stories or gives them a slant to favor their own peculiar biases. This censorship has gone so far that even controlled studies of the press, where news reporters were handed factual stories and asked to rewrite them in their own words have clearly revealed their biases.[7] Censorship is a fact of American life.

---

7 See S. Robert Lichter, Linda Lichter and Stanley Rothman, *The Media Elite; America's New Power Brokers*,

However, the censorship of modern times is not usually a censorship imposed by the government on the press, but self-censorship. The press reports stories or refuses to report them based on its own ideological bias.

To understand why the press probably won't censor panicky stories about the millenium bug, it is important to understand how the press and the leftist establishment in general thinks. The power base of the left is composed of "clients". These clients are people and groups who are beneficiaries of the leftist agenda. These clients are given various benefits, ranging from government payments to political clout. They in turn support the leftist establishment with their votes and their voices. Examples of clients of the left range from blacks to homosexuals, and from welfare recipients and environmentalists to social security recipients. Understand that these client groups are clients of the left, not just of government. The leftists in government naturally support their clients with benefits. However, the leftists in the press (and the mainstream press is predominantly populated by leftists) also support the same clients with selective reporting.[8]

This client-based selective reporting is at the heart of modern censorship. The press will tend to report stories in a light favorable to its clients, and disfavorable to its anti-clients. Thus, for example, the press might report a homosexual rights protest with favorable remarks about the homosexuals (clients), while calling the Christians (anti-clients) opposed to it homophobes, hate mongers, and the like. Or, as another example, they might report

---

(Adler and Adler, Bethesda, Maryland, 1986) as well as the analysis of their data in Lawrence Dawson, *The Death of Reality*, (The Paradigm Co., Boise, Idaho: 1997) p.80.

8 Op. Cit., *The Death of Reality*, pp. 73-101.

The Great Media Scare   51

an environmental issue by positioning the environmentalists (clients) as the good guys and big business (anti-clients) as the bad guys, while ignoring all the people who will lose their jobs as a result of some new regulation.

Considering the millenium bug from this standpoint, it should be clear that it is bad news to an anti-client of the left: business. As such, the press probably would not engage in self-censorship concerning the bug. Quite to the contrary, this may be reason to report things as worse than they really are, and make the scare bigger.

On the other hand, the bug also has the potential to cause lots of trouble for the government, which is currently under an administration with which the press is sympathetic. Will the press censor news about the bug on these grounds?

The answer is a resolute no! A media-driven scare concerning the millenium bug will be highly advantageous to those who wish to enlarge the powers of government. It will provide a means to advance their plans for radical change at a much more rapid pace than would usually be possible. This will become evident in the chapters to come. As such, the government will probably make no attempt to silence the press or keep it from reporting on the bug. It will ask no favors. If anything, the government may actually encourage such reporting.

Finally, even if some move were made to censor the millenium bug story, censorship is becoming practically impossible in the modern world. With the advent of desktop publishing, many people of all different persuasions are publishing newsletters. More and more people are turning to these newsletters as sources of information because they know full well that the press doesn't tell them the truth about a lot of things. The internet is also growing into an information resource that is quite beyond the ability of government to censor in any detailed way. One can easily log on to the internet, do a search on "millenium bug" or "year 2000 problem" and come up with tons of first-hand information about what's happening. Because of these technology-driven changes in how people are getting information, any self-censorship or government censorship of the mainline press may only succeed in driving people to these "underground" sources to learn the truth.

If censorship drives people to "underground" sources, it could actually heighten the panic. Underground media sources are rarely so reserved in their prognostications as the mainstream press. For example, while *Newsweek* is telling its readers that it might be wise to stuff a little cash in the mattress, *Strategic Investment*, a financial newsletter with an internationalist and libertarian perspective, is telling its readers that President Clinton may be happy to let the millenium bug cause a national emergency so he can cancel elections and take a third term in office for himself.[9] The internet may be even less reserved. And if people catch on to the fact that the mainstream press is self-consciously censoring the story, they'll really panic.

As such, censorship appears to be both highly unlikely and potentially counterproductive.

---

9   James Dale Davidson, *Strategic Investment*, August 20, 1997.

6. Risk and Reward Basics

As time goes on and organizations fail to deal with the problems in their software, more and more people will realize that these antiquated programs will still be running when the millenium flips. So, the question ceases to become whether the software will be fixed in time—because it won't be—but rather, what's going to happen when software that can't handle the new millenium leaps into the new millenium anyway?

The trouble is, nobody knows for sure how serious those problems will be. More people are starting to get scared as they consider what *might* happen, but nobody knows what really *will* happen.

However, the way people will respond to the threat of trouble is *very predictable*. Simply put, they will remove themselves from the way of trouble to the best of their ability. The more daring will put up with a certain amount of risk, provided they are appropriately rewarded for it. *This simple fact is absolutely central to understanding the impact that the millenium bug is going to have on society in the next few years.*

Accurately assaying the impact of the technical problems the bug will create *is not the issue*. Knowing beforehand whether the computers are going to give us a few easily fixed glitches, or whether they are going to shut down the world would be nice, but nobody seems to be able to figure that out.

The fact that nobody seems to be able to accurately assess the technical impact of the bug, however, means that its secondary, social impact is virtually certain. *The unknown technical impact means that there is a real risk involved.* People and markets will respond to this risk.

According to Webster's Dictionary[1], a risk is "the chance of injury, damage or loss." The millenium bug is introducing a certain amount of risk into financial markets, banking, payment systems, and life support systems. Risk is not damage or loss, just the *chance* of it. That is exactly what the millenium bug will introduce into the global economy.

People respond to risk—the chance of damage or loss—in a very predictable way. That applies to the average Joe-on-the-street and it applies to the sophisticated Wall Street investor. In the absence of a payback for taking a risk, people avoid that risk to the best of their ability. They can, however, be induced to take some risk by being offered a reward for it.

The bond market is a classic example of how risk works. A bond is merely a financial arrangement whereby someone lends someone else money for a period of time, in exchange for interest on that money. Typically, the interest rate, or the amount one is paid for lending the money, is based on risk. For example, US Treasury obligations are considered to be relatively low risk. The main risk factor is simply inflation of the currency.[2] Thus, T-Bills pay a relatively low rate of interest when inflation is low. Municipal bonds carry

---

1 Webster's New World Dictionary, Second College Edition, (Simon and Schuster:1980).
2 At least as far as most polite investors, who are willing to buy government obligations, are concerned.

Risk and Reward Basics 55

more risk because municipalities do occasionally go under (though the bonds are often secured by hidden liens on all of the property in the district). People are induced to take this small additional risk by being offered better interest rates, and possible tax exemptions. Corporate bonds carry more risk still, depending on the issuer, and they again pay higher interest to compensate for the risk. Typically, bond issuers are rated by an outside agency to tell potential investors how much risk is involved. A big profitable company that is certain to be around in the coming years—AT&T for example—will get a high rating. A relatively new company that has yet to make a profit will get a low rating.

In short, the bond market rewards risk-taking with *higher interest rates.*

Now, from a purely technical point of view, one might think that all the risk of the millenium bug is concentrated on January 1, 2000 and possibly a week, or perhaps even a few months of trouble following. Come the end of that first week in the new millenium, we will all have a much clearer picture of where we stand.

So in terms of the technical difficulties of the millenium bug, investors, businessmen and ordinary people will want to protect their assets in the period of December 31, 1999 to January 3, 2000[3]. *Free markets are going to have to reflect this risk.*

This is very important to understand, so let me drive that statement home: *Free markets are going to have to reflect this risk.* This is the crux of the real danger of the millenium bug.

---

[3] December 31, 1999 falls on a Friday, so January 3, 2000 is the following Monday.

To see why this fact is so important, consider a bank account offering a 5% *per anum* interest rate. Four days of interest amounts to 0.0535%. In other words, a $10,000 investment will be rewarded with $5.35 during the usual four-day period. Normally, such a small reward is acceptable because the risk that that bank will fold in any given 4-day period is small, and even then, the FDIC insures the deposit. However, it does not make any sense to accept a paltry reward of $5.35 on a $10,000 investment when that $10,000 could be at risk of total loss when the bank fails because all of its customers are driven away by an inability to make payments because of millenium bugs. The sensible thing to do in the face of such a risk/reward equation would be to withdraw one's money from the bank and re-deposit it after the turn of the new year.

Just looking at this simple fact of risk/reward in the banking system, we can conclude that one of three things is *certain* to happen come the turn of the millenium. Either:

1) People will withdraw their money from the banks, or
2) Interest rates will go up dramatically to compensate depositors for their increased risk, or
3) The government will intervene.

None of these scenarios is terribly desirable.

The fractional reserve banking system adds another dimension to the problem. Everyone knows in the back of their mind that if too many people run to the bank on December 31, 1999 to withdraw all their money, the banks aren't going to be able to provide the necessary cash. Because of the way the fractional reserve banking system works, the money just won't be there for everybody to withdraw when they want to. To be one of the

Risk and Reward Basics

select few who can protect yourself this way, you'll have to beat your neighbors to the bank. So when will you want to go withdraw your money? On December 30? December 15? May 23? The point is this: *the fractional reserve banking system will drive the risk backward in time* since people who realize that the year 2000 glitch poses a problem too late in the game won't be able to protect themselves.

Secondly, *the fractional reserve banking system will multiply the risk greatly* because only a small percentage of panicky people are capable of upsetting the whole system.

The technical problem will occur in a moment of time. Anticipation of the technical problem is going to cause trouble long before the ball at Times Square falls. How long will people dare to keep their money in the bank? How long will they hold their life insurance policies? their mutual funds? their stocks? their government bonds? When people start deciding to take cover, a panic could ensue that would crash the whole system overnight.

Don't make the mistake of thinking this is just some Chicken Little "the sky is falling" scenario. Bankers are professional risk managers. They are continually looking at loan applications and evaluating the risks of various propositions. Bankers who recognize that the millenium bug is a problem are *already* factoring it into the risk equation for loans they are making. For example, David Iacino, senior manager at the $60 billion Bank of Boston testified before the Senate Banking, Housing and Urban Affairs Committee that[4]

---

4 Testimony of July 10, 1997. (At http://www.senate.gov).

"Credit policy is being reviewed to account for the potential risk that the borrower's ability to repay outstanding debt may be affected by the impact of the year 2000 on the borrower. Increased allowances for potential loan losses are accordingly being evaluated. Existing loans . . . are being watched in the event that the customer's own millenium preparation expense may erode comfortable profit margins."

The Federal Reserve is also advising banks to factor the impact of the millenium bug into the lending process:[5]

"Corporate customers who have not considered Year 2000 issues may experience a disruption in business, resulting in financial difficulties that could negatively influence their creditworthiness. Examiners now verify that a bank incorporates a borrower's Year 2000 preparedness into its underwriting standards, and that loan officers assess the extent of Year 2000 computer problems that may influence a borrower's ability to repay its loans on a timely basis."

In other words, professional risk managers are already accounting for the problem and planning to adjust for "potential loan losses" and customers who "experience a disruption in business."

Just how big of a problem will these professional risk managers uncover as they begin to analyze the potential for losses as a result of the millenium bug?

---

[5] Testimony of Governor Edward W. Kelley, Jr. before the Subcommittee on Financial Services and Technology, U.S. Senate, July 30, 1997. See also the May 5, 1997 press release from the Federal Financial Institutions Examination Council (a part of the Federal Reserve).

Risk and Reward Basics

Normally, banks and insurance companies are experts at calculating actual risks in a precise fashion. Their businesses depend on it, so they have invested a good deal in systems and methods to determine risk. A bank will quote you a rate for a loan based on current interest rates, what the loan is for, and your credit history. They have plenty of statistical data to tell them what their risks in making the loan are.

The problem with the millenium bug is that it is a wild card. Nobody really knows what its effect will be, and nobody will until the day it hits. There are no statistics from the last turn of the century to tell professional money managers what the risks will be. The only thing anybody will have to go on is what the "experts" think will happen.

Year 2000 experts are predicting that perhaps 5% of all businesses will fail because of the millenium bug.[6] Such a figure may seem extreme, but these are the numbers being quoted by the media right now. Such figures could actually soar as the countdown continues and more and more businesses realize that they aren't going to make the deadline, or that the cost of making the deadline will run them into the ground before they ever reach the millenium.

One has to remember that many businesses today have stretched and strained to remove every last bit of unproductive fat so that they can compete with cheap foreign goods flooding the market and squeeze out every last bit of earnings for their shareholders. Even so, many have very poor earnings, and many are laden with debt

---

6 "The Day the World Shuts Down," *Newsweek*, June 2, 1997, p.58

that must be serviced every month. The problem is, year 2000 preparations are an essentially unproductive activity. They tie up resources that could be used to produce profits and growth instead. This simple fact tends to push businesses that are already operating on slim profit margins to ignore the problem. They simply cannot afford to deal with it. That may be shortsighted and foolish, but it appears to be happening.

In any event, a 5% failure rate may not be a pie-in-the-sky number put forth by somebody who stands to profit from the scare. As a rule, businesses that cannot afford to resolve their year 2000 problems will not deal with them before the millenium change. Only once they have been hit will they start to fix the problem. Of course they must then add the expense of fixing the bugs to the expense of the trouble they are causing. And generally fixing something before it breaks is less expensive than fixing it after it has broken. Barring a miracle, businesses that can't afford to fix the millenium bug now won't be able to fix it in the year 2000.

In reality, 5% is a huge number, and it would have a tremendous impact on interest rates. Look at it this way: suppose you have $1 million to lend. You are paying the people who lent you the money 5% and you're lending at 9% under normal circumstances. If you lend for one year on these terms to 20 people, $50,000 each, your profit is $40,000, provided you have no defaults. One default would devour that profit and leave you with a $10,000 loss, unless the loan was secured, in which case you might recover the money by selling whatever secured it.

Now a 5% millenium bug failure rate means that one of those 20 people will probably default, in addition to the normal risk of default due to other factors. That means you'll have to build an additional $50,000 of profit

Risk and Reward Basics

into your loans in order to compensate for the loss. In other words, you'll have to lend at a 14% rate, not a 9% rate. Neither does this factor in the risk of those who are lending you the money to begin with. If they are smart, they will realize that you have a 5% chance of failing, and they'll want to be compensated for that risk. Fail to do it, and they won't loan you the money. So you'll have to pay your depositors 10% and charge 19% for the loan, just to maintain your usual profit margin.

More generally speaking, an analysis like this gives a nice little formula for how failure rates would affect interest rates. If F is the failure rate of businesses due to the millenium bug and R is the interest rate increase on a loan, while T is the term of the loan in years, then

$$R = 2F/T$$

In the above example, $T = 1$ year, $F = 5\%$, which causes a rate increase R of 10%. Obviously, short-term loans are most affected by this risk. Even an anticipated 1% failure rate would boost 90-day rates by 8%. For either of these examples, the resulting rate increases are huge. Such rate hikes would devastate a heavily indebted economy in very short order.

Now, obviously our analysis here is somewhat simplified. Bankers can, for example, reduce their risk by lending only to companies that are prepared internally for the millenium bug. None the less, that risk cannot be eliminated. Companies are interdependent on each other. Even a company that fixes all its computers has a myriad of suppliers and customers that it must depend on. The only place we could be going wrong is in overestimating the failure rate of businesses. Even if 5% is an overestimate, we have to wonder how far over it is, and how anyone is going to determine that it is way too high. Bankers, after all, tend to be conservative people, but conservative in a way that reduces their risk. If one expert says the failure rate will be 5% and another says it will only be 0.5% who will the banker listen to? If they guy who says 0.5% doesn't have a much better analysis, the banker will take the higher figure, and plan accordingly. He'd be a fool not to.

And then there is the problem that banks normally borrow money for very short time periods. Thus, T in our equation above tends toward zero. As such, even a very small failure rate can mandate a large interest rate increase to keep depositors happy. That will be the real problem the banking industry has to face.

Don't think for a minute that this possibility is merely the idea of one writer. Big-time investors are already catching on to the possibility. December 1999 futures contracts that leverage interest rates are already becoming a hot item among hedge funds. The approach being taken is a so-called "butterfly spread," where the investor sells December 1999 contracts and buys September 2000 and March 2000 contracts. Most of this activity is taking place in eurodollar and euromark contracts, with over $5 billion in contracts already sold. In short, more than a few sophisticated investors are betting on an interest rate spike around the turn of the millenium.

The rest of this book is dedicated to examining this little-pondered dimension of the millenium bug. In the following pages we will examine the likely dynamics of the scare that is brewing. We will discuss the fallout of the scare, which will probably include ballooning interest rates, the threat of a banking panic, and government intervention. Neither will we content ourselves with vague generalizations. Rather, we'll look at numbers, statistics and facts to draw conclusions.

7. How the Banking System Works

When people start to get scared about the millenium bug, at least some are going to start taking steps to protect themselves. One of those steps might be to withdraw money from their bank. When major media like Newsweek has already suggested it, 2½ years in advance, *we must take the possibility seriously*. Many are bound to heed such advice. And the banking system is extremely vulnerable to this kind of a response. It has also, historically, been subject to such disruptions from time to time.

If we want to quantitatively understand what will happen to the banking system as a result of the millenium bug, the first step is to understand how a bank works.

Basically, a bank receives deposits from people who have money and lends it back out to people who need money. The bank makes money by charging more to lend the money than it pays to depositors. To maximize profits and encourage deposits, banks normally borrow money from depositors short-term and lend it out long-term.

This practice of borrowing short and lending long necessitates a fiction that just about everybody who deposits money into a bank buys into. This is the simple idea that when one deposits money in a bank, the money is somehow "in" that bank.

Consider a basic 30-year fixed rate mortgage for example. A bank that did not engage in this fiction would offer a 30-year fixed rate Certificate of Deposit that had a repayment schedule similar to the mortgage. Lenders would buy these CDs whereby the bank would accumulate principle to lend to borrowers who want a 30-year mortgage. The Certificates of Deposit would not generally be redeemable by bank customers ahead of schedule, unless the bank had other customers willing to buy them. They would represent a commitment by a bank's customers to tie up their funds.

Banks don't do this today for two basic reasons: first and foremost, more people are interested in borrowing long term than in lending long term. As such, if the bank only lent long term against the long-term deposits it had, it would not be able to make nearly enough long-term loans to fulfill the demand for them. It would have to pass up lots of money making opportunities. Second, the bank can pay its depositors less interest by borrowing money short term because the short-term loan carries less risk. This generally increases the bank's profit margin.

The ultimate short-term deposit that banks offer is the so-called demand account. A checking account, which offers no interest, or a demand-type savings account, which offers a very modest return gives the bank the widest profit margin. A checking account with $10,000 in it means a bank can lend out nearly $10,000 at an 8% or 9% rate, and make $800 or $900 per year in interest. A $10,000 5-year CD that pays 5% represents only a profit of $300 or $400. These demand accounts, however, propagate the fiction that one has money "in the bank."

Most people, if pressed to acknowledge the truth, understand that the bank takes the money they deposit and lends it to other people. It isn't really "in" the bank

How the Banking System Works   65

at all; it's out on loan. Yet people do not think this way on a day-in, day-out basis. Banks are able to maintain the fiction of money being "in the bank" by maintaining a certain reserve against deposits. Normally, demand depositors don't all come calling for their money at the same time, so it suffices to keep a percentage of all deposits available in cash to cover demands made by those depositors in any given time period.

Typically, a bank will try to hold the amount kept in reserve against depositor demands to an absolute minimum. Reserves typically don't earn interest because they aren't being lent out, so excessive reserves represent lost income to the bank. For example, if a bank had $200 million in deposits and reserves 50% of deposits, and depositors were being paid 5% and money was being lent at 10%, the bank would make no money at all. In the same situation with 1% reserves, the bank would make $9,800,000 on the deal. So banks naturally want to minimize the amount of reserves they keep.

At present, all banks in the United States are licensed by the United States government and controlled by the Federal Reserve Board. Similar regulations apply in different countries, where banks are typically licensed and controlled either directly by governments, or by a central bank of some kind.

The Federal Reserve Board, and other central bank regulators, maintain reserve requirements for banks. These reserve requirements typically take the form of a minimum percentage of deposits to be held in reserve. If a bank falls below the required level, it can be subject to disciplinary action.

By borrowing money through demand accounts and lending it out long-term, banks effectively create money. To see this, imagine a simplified economy, which consists of three people and a bank. Person A opens an account at the bank in the amount of $10,000. Suppose the reserve ratio is 50%. The bank now has $5000 to lend, which it lends to Person B. Person B buys goods and services from Person C, who receives the $5000 from Person B, and promptly deposits it into his account at the bank. Now there is $15,000 in the bank, and the bank can lend an additional $2500. Again it lends Person B the $2500. At this point in the game, there is supposedly $17,500 circulating in the economy, even though there was only $10,000 to begin with. The other $7500 is purely fictitious. It is created by the fiction that Person A has $10,000 in the bank and Person B has $5000 in the bank. The reality is that the bank has $7500 in reserve, and Person B has $2500 on loan. However, as long as everyone agrees that the bank deposit is as good as cash, the game can go on. Person A can say he has $10,000, Person B can say he has $5000 and Person C can say he has $2500.

In real life, the game is much more complex because there are multitudes of players, but the essence of it is still the same. The mathematical formula for how much money M can be created by a new deposit N given a reserve ratio r is given by

$$M = (N \Sigma(1-r)^n)-N = N/r - N$$

This formula is really very simple. In our example above, the reserve ratio was 50%, or r=0.50, and N was $10,000, so the amount of money created would be

$$M = \$10,000/_{0.50} - \$10,000 = \$10,000$$

In practice, reserve ratios are very small. When the ratios get small, banks effectively create a tremendous amount of money out of thin air from new deposits. Thus, for example, with a reserve ratio of 1%, a bank will create

How the Banking System Works 67

some $990,000 of new money for every $10,000 deposited. Decreasing the reserve ratio even a little bit can likewise result in a tremendous creation of new money. Thus, for example, changing a reserve ratio from 1% to ½% will result in the creation of $1,000,000 in new money.

The key to understanding this system is that it works rationally, with mathematical precision, as long as the money supply and reserve ratios can be controlled. In our model economy that had only $10,000 to begin with, the banking system could create another $10,000 given a reserve ratio of 50%, but once that had been achieved, it could not create any more. To create more money, either (a) more real money had to come into the system from somewhere or (b) the reserve requirements had to be lowered. As such, the fictitious money supply cannot go ballooning out of control as long as these factors are kept under control.

We could, of course, complicate the picture I have outlined here by the fact that the money issued in most modern countries is itself tied into the banking system, rather than being specie-based like gold or silver coin, or notes representing gold or silver holdings in some vault. However, it is not necessary to complicate our picture of the banking system with that. The fractional reserve system we have outlined here does not require printing-press money to work. It could work just as easily with a gold standard. And the consequences of the millenium bug for the banking system will be the same.

8. The Anatomy of a Banking Collapse

The fractional reserve system generally works well for a bank as long as the perceived risk of depositing money with a bank is low. Problems arise when, for one reason or another, short-term depositors believe that they are not being rewarded sufficiently for their risks. Since a bank borrows short and lends long, the bank can get into trouble when the perceived risk increases suddenly. Perceived risk can increase suddenly for any number of reasons, and it can be directed at a specific financial institution or at the industry as a whole.

One of the most common reasons that perceived risk increases suddenly is growing inflation. Nobody wants to keep money in a bank account that is losing money because the inflation rate is higher than the interest rate paid on the account. It doesn't make any sense. The obvious solution for the bank is to raise the rate it pays its customers. This is the natural, market-oriented solution that a bank can apply to compensate for any kind of increase in risk. A better payback can compensate people for a greater risk.

However, since a bank normally lends long and borrows short, the rate it can pay its depositors has practical limits. For example, suppose a bank has all of its money lent out at 8.5% on 30-year mortgages because inflation has been running around 3% for ever so long. Then inflation spikes up toward 10%, and depositors require 12% to keep their money in the bank. Now the bank is in trouble. To keep its depositors, it must take a 3.5% loss on all the money it borrows from depositors. A bank cannot do this day-in and day-out for very long. So it must either keep the rates it pays depositors down to a profitable level, or try to increase its inventory of high-rate loans to cover the losing ones.

If the risk of keeping one's money in the bank grows slowly, banks can generally cope with it by increasing the rates they pay depositors, and rolling over low rate loans for higher rate loans. However, if that (real or imagined) risk grows quickly, a bank can face a run. In such a situation, short-term depositors seek to recover their deposits, although the deposits are tied up in long term loans, and the bank's cash reserve is quickly depleted. At this point, the bank can no longer satisfy depositors' demands, and the fiction that one "has money in the bank" is exploded. It does a bank little good to try to entice depositors to keep their accounts open in such a situation. In the middle of a panic, practically nobody will be induced to take a risk, no matter how great the reward. Rates could be 100% per day and it would not be enough in the middle of a real panic.

In this situation, one of three things can happen:

> **1)** The bank can start calling loans. Although most loans are for a fixed period of time, a bank can normally call that loan and require the principal to be paid in full, immediately. Many loans have such a clause in the loan agreement. If the borrower cannot repay, the bank can auction off the collateral for that loan to raise cash to repay borrowers.

The Anatomy of a Banking Collapse

2) The bank can close its doors and hope the panic will subside soon.

3) The bank can seek government intervention.

Normally, all three of these things will happen at once in a major banking confidence crisis. They all happened at once in 1933. Many banks had to close their doors. Many banks were calling loans. And in response to the need of the banking industry, Franklin D. Roosevelt declared a banking holiday, effectively took the country off the gold standard, and established federal insurance of bank deposits in order to stem the panic.

Now, of course, government intervention is built into the banking system through Federal Reserve control of the banking industry, and federal insurance through the FDIC. This has greatly reduced the potential for bank runs on individual banks as well as the system as a whole. However, such insurance programs may not always prevent a run on the system. That depends on the nature of the sudden risk that was causing a panic. If that risk was of such a nature that it drew into question the ability of the insurance programs to pay up in a timely fashion or return payment in "real" money, the banking system as a whole could still face a run.

Now, with this basic understanding of the banking system and how banks get into trouble, let's go on to see how the millenium bug could affect the banking system.

The Millenium Bug

9. The Millenium Bug Bank Panic

The real danger of the millenium bug to the banking system is not the technical problem, but the banking system itself. Fractional reserve banking could turn a small but reasonable risk which could be compensated for into an out-and-out panic.

If banks borrowed money for the same terms that they lend it on, they could gracefully compensate for the risks people have to take around the turn of the millenium. The interest rate for a CD that crossed the millenium boundary could reflect the increased risk due to the millenium bug. Averaged over a 5-year or maybe even a 30-year maturity, the risk due to the bug would be almost insignificant. It would add a fraction of a percentage point to the rate of the CD. However, because a bank borrows short and lends long, *and* much of the risk due to the millenium bug is concentrated in a very short period of time, banks could face a crunch. In the absence of suitable rewards, short-term borrowers will want out. The myth of having "money in the bank" will evaporate as borrowers cannot get out, and we will be faced with a full-scale, worldwide bank run.

Let's look at the banking system today and put some hard numbers behind this assertion that the millenium bug will precipitate a bank run.

As we've discussed, the Federal Reserve regulates the reserve requirements for bank deposits. The requirements are spelled out in so-called "Regulation D". Although somewhat complicated, this regulation is worth reviewing as a starting point to understanding the leveraging of the banking system.

Firstly, the regulation breaks accounts up into two categories, so-called *transaction accounts*, and *time deposit accounts*. Transaction accounts include checking accounts and NOW accounts, as well as savings accounts which allow automatic transfers or ATM transfers, or an unlimited number of telephone transfers each month. Time deposit accounts include Certificates of Deposit with a maturity of at least 7 days, as well as savings accounts which allow the institution to require at least 7 days notice before withdrawal (although the institution need not requre such notice).

All time deposits are subject to a zero reserve requirement. Transaction accounts are subject to a 3% reserve requirement on "the first $54 million of net transactions balances and 10% of the rest." However, there is no reserve requirement on the first $4.2 million, as an aid to smaller financial institutions.

The details of these reserve requirements tend to blur the picture of how leveraged banks really are due to the fractional reserve system. To get an accurate picture, one has to take a look at money supply figures. The broadest money supply figure published by the Federal Reserve, called M3, includes all currency, and all demand and time deposits. From this figure, one should subtract the money market deposits (which are not bank deposits) and the actual currency to get a picture of the total money in the banking system. This can be compared to the reserves maintained by the banks under Regulation D.

The Millenium Bug Bank Panic

In May, 1997, M3 was $5,071.7 billion,[1] and the money market component of it was $878.8 billion. The currency component was $406.1 billion. That means bank deposits were $3,786.8 billion. The total reserves maintained by the banks, on the other hand, were $45.019 billion. Thus, the effective reserve ratio is

$$\$45.019 / \$3786.8 = 0.01189$$

or about 1.2% for the whole system. This number is what a combination of government requirements in the form of Regulation D and market forces in the form of interest rates create.

Another way of putting this figure is that for every new $100 deposited in a bank, the banking system creates $\$100/0.01189 = \$8410.43$ in "money" which circulates through the banking system. In other words there are depositors out there with account balances of one form

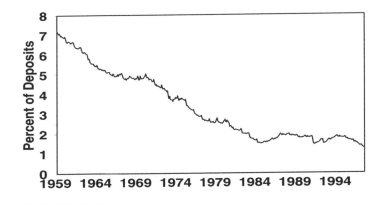

Fig. 1: Bank Reserves as a percentage of deposits.

---

1 Federal Reserve Board of Governors data.

or another which state that they hold $8410.43 in assets, while the bank has only $100 in reserve to pay them.

The effective reserve ratio is a measure of how leveraged the banking system is. This leverage increases profits for the banking system, but it also dramatically increases the danger due to panics. You can think of it similarly to a mortgage. If you buy a house for $100,000 cash, and the house goes down in value by 10%, you lost 10% of your money. If it goes up 10% then you made 10%. On the other hand, if you buy a house for $2,000 down and a 98% loan, then a $10,000 price change means that either you made 500% or you owe the bank $8000 and can't pay.

In the same way, when people systematically start pulling money out of the bank and stuffing it in their mattresses, the bank quickly comes to a point where it can't pay them. Under normal economic conditions this does not happen. People respond statistically to gradual changes in the economy. If they are making more money than they need, they slowly accumulate excesses. If they aren't making as much as they need, they slowly draw on their accumulations. Likewise, massive investment opportunities, like the great bull stock market, can cause people to withdraw from savings to participate in those opportunities. From month to month, a bank's reserves change slowly. In the past few years, reserves have been decreasing while deposits have been increasing. In such a situation, either banks must maintain their reserves by retiring more loans than they initiate, or the government must create money and ease up on reserve requirements (which is what they have been doing).

While the system can handle a gradual change in reserves by properly managing its loans, it cannot handle a sudden shock. For example, if 0.6% of all bank deposits were withdrawn in a short period of time, banks would

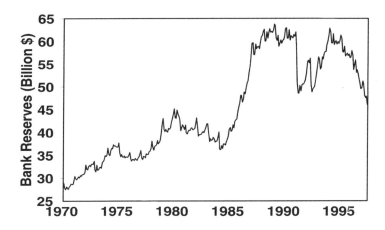

Fig. 2: Bank reserves in dollars.

not have sufficient reserves to meet central bank requirements. If people attempted to withdraw 1.2% of all deposits, the banks would close their doors and start sending people home empty-handed. The banks could attempt to call loans in a desperate attempt to raise cash, but that would probably only result in bankruptcy filings and auctions that would take months if not years to carry through to completion. In other words, banks would close their doors or cry for government intervention—probably both at the same time.

Is it realistic to suggest that a millenium bug scare will result in 1.2% or more of all bank deposits being withdrawn? Let's look at the figures a little more carefully to see what such a possibility really entails.

First, out of $3786.8 billion in total deposits, some $648.4 billion are demand deposits (checking accounts) and $1318.5 billion are savings accounts. Most of the balance is time deposits (e.g. CDs with a maturity of 7 or more days). If we just consider the demand deposits and savings accounts, then there would be $45.019 billion in reserves for $1966.9 billion in deposits. This gives a reserve ratio of 2.28% against all deposits which people normally think of as being immediately available for use. Of course, it ignores the fact that some of the CDs with short maturities could be redeemed before the millenium if a panic started brewing. To be more conservative still, we could just apply the reserves to demand deposits. Even then, the reserve ratio is a mere 6.94%.

To sum these figures up, if

1) 1.2% of all bank deposits, or
2) 2.3% of all checking and savings deposits, or
3) 7% of all checking deposits

were suddenly withdrawn from the banking system, then the banks would run dry of money and be forced to close their doors.

One ought to conclude from these numbers that the banking system is very vulnerable to a panic. It is not at all unreasonable to think that such percentages could be *easily* met and surpassed if an all-out media scare about the millenium bug develops. The last few months of 1999 could get real ugly for banks, as people start trying to anticipate the bug and get out of harm's way by taking their money out of the bank. Only a few percent have to get scared enough to act in order to cause major problems. Will that happen? You consider the facts and decide for yourself:

1) The banks will provide little incentive for "captive" depositors to trust them with their money across the millenium change.

The Millenium Bug Bank Panic

2) People will become acutely alert to the risks of the millenium bug in late 1999 as the media covers it more and more.

3) Banks are highly leveraged, and only a small fraction of people need to lose trust in them to cause a basic failure of the whole system.

4) Even people who don't think the millenium bug will be a problem could lose trust in the banking system because they know it's highly leveraged and that a few people who are afraid of the millenium bug could ruin it.

Why, indeed, should people trust such a highly leveraged system that appears to be at significant risk when they are offered no reasonable incentive to?

Perhaps it should be no surprise that central bankers are quietly aware of the potential for such a banking collapse. In a private conversation one European central banker admitted that they were developing sophisticated computerized economic models of the situation to anticpate exactly such a scenario and deal with it.

To avert such a collapse, the banking industry needs to do two things:

1) Minimize the risks involved by working hard to solve their year 2000 problems, and

2) Reward depositors for taking the risk of depositing funds during the problem period.

If banks don't do these two things, they're in trouble. Right now, it is too early in the game to determine definitively what *will* happen. We can only make educated guesses and watch what develops.

One thing we can say for certain is that if bank runs happen, they will occur *before* the turn of the millenium. By the evening of December 31, 1999 people will have done all that they feel is necessary to prepare for the bug. That will include withdrawing their money from the bank. Once the millenium turns, every bank will show its hand, and people will be able to return their money to those who have successfully dealt with their computer problems, and survived the bank run.

Understanding that a bank run will occur *before* the turn of the millenium (and not after) is crucial to understanding how events will be played out when it does happen. We will dig into this more deeply in coming chapters.

A Word About the FDIC

We should also discuss the FDIC, since most people think it somehow insures banks so that their money is safe even if their bank collapses. The Federal Deposit Insurance Corporation, or FDIC, was created during the depression to insure banks. This federal agency supposedly makes banks safe against bank runs, because the depositors are insured.

Unfortunately, the FDIC will be of little use in stemming the tide of bank runs in 1999. Understand that the FDIC merely maintains electronic deposits that can be used to bail out banks when they default. When a bank defaults and the FDIC steps in, you won't find a g-man in a pinstripe suit standing in the bank's lobby handing out cash to depositors.

Standard operating procedure with the FDIC is to liquidate the assets of a bank, selling the loans to other banks, etc., and paying out the depositors. Alternatively, they might arrange a merger with a healthier bank. In

The Millenium Bug Bank Panic 81

either case, a depositor at a failing institution is only compensated with an account deposit at another institution. In the case of a merger, the depositor is just handed a new account book with the same deposit he had originally. If a bank is liquidated, the depositor gets a check which he can deposit somewhere else.

While such an approach makes perfect sense in the case when one bank collapses because of bad management or whatever, it won't work at all when people are trying to escape from the electronic money system as a whole, and demanding cash. If you want cash paper money, and your bank can't give it to you, the FDIC will no more be able to give it to you. The best they'll do is give you a check—perhaps after a few months—which you can take to another bank and experience the same problem all over again.

In short, while the FDIC may do a fine job protecting depositors when a single institution defaults, its mechanisms are completely useless to defend against systemic collapse, which is exactly what the millenium bug will cause. It may seem ridiculous that an institution which was devised during a period of systemic collapse to protect the system is going to be completely incapable of protecting it from a systemic collapse, but that is the way things are shaping up.

Don't Get Caught

No matter what the government does, or what you might think about a cashless society, you don't want to get caught in that 98.8% who don't get their money out of the bank in time. You don't want a large degree of uncertainty like that in your life, even if it only lasts for a week. You won't sleep at night. You won't think straight. If you hate the idea of a cashless society, getting caught in the bank run will all but force you to accept it. If you couldn't care less about a cashless society, then you'll miss the opportunity of a lifetime by being caught with the masses in the run.

The only way to avoid getting caught is to anticipate the bank run far in advance. Now I'll be honest with you here, a year ago, I thought "far in advance" would mean mid-1999. Yet as I've watched the media coverage of this crisis grow month by month, and I've watched people get more and more alarmed, I've come to realize that the crisis could occur any day. After all, 1.2% isn't very much.

Don't think for a second that anyone is going to tell you the bank runs have started. The government won't want you to panic. The bankers won't want you to panic. They'll try to keep the media tight-lipped. Your neighbors and friends won't tell you either. They'll be down at the bank in line in front of you. In fact, the bleeding may have already begun before you read this. I know for a fact that Gary North has been advising his newsletter subscribers to pull their money out of the bank slowly and quietly, and at least some of them have got to be doing it.[2] How many more, especially programmers and the like (who know what's going on), are moving carefully and quietly to protect themselves? How much does it take to become significant? Go back and look at the graph of bank reserves. Why are they falling so?

Now, if you're anything like me, dropping your bank account down to a bare minimum isn't all that easy. Most of us are already very dependent on electronic entries in computers for our money. We pay bills with checks. We

---

2 *Remnant Review*, January and February, 1998.

The Millenium Bug Bank Panic

use credit cards. We aren't used to stuffing cash in the matress, and we consider it unsafe (and it is if you have very much). So you're going to have to change your habits to avoid the initial bank run. Realistically, that will probably take you some time. I recommend you set monthly goals to get your bank accounts down to the point that they contain no more than needed to cover a month's living expenses. Take them down further than that if you can manage it. Write those goals down today. Don't wait. What do you have to lose? A few percent per anum? Is that really worth the risk, even if this whole thing blows over? I don't think so.

Please don't become complacent about this. It is all too easy to read what's written here and agree with it, but then to get caught up in our day to day activities and forget it. Then you'll only be reminded of it when it hits the newspapers, and that's too late. A recent survey by *Information Week* magazine, a leading computer industry weekly, polled 1100 information technology professionals—people who know how bad this thing is—and 38% said "they may withdraw personal assets from banks and investment companies before the year 2000."[3] That right there is enough to make the bank runs history. *Don't become complacent.*

Monitoring the Situation

When exactly bank runs occur will depend in large part on the publicity given to the millenium bug. There is likely to be a certain point at which the publicity starts reaching critical mass, and some people start to move quietly.

---

[3] *Information Week*, November 10, 1997.

While I don't recommend you try to watch the situation in the hope of beating a bank run, watching the situation develop might give you an edge on using some of the strategies discussed later in this book to make some quick money off of it.

There are two things to watch: one is bank reserves. When you see reserves taking a nose dive, it's the eleventh hour, and high time to get out. Don't assume you'll have enough warning to see the numbers before you make a decision, though. Watch the media too. If they start telling people to take their money out of the bank, then make sure you're the first one in line. The next thing to watch is the banking industry's progress toward solving their year 2000 problems. To do this you'll have to read between the lines a bit. The industry and government will generally put the best spin they can on things, so don't let that spin deceive you. Learn to see through it. A good thing to watch is deadlines. Have they slipped? Look at statistics for the industry. Have 99% achieved compliance? Have 30%? Is the industry as a whole going to meet the final deadline? Watch whether what is meant by "compliance" changes with time in an effort to claim everyone's ready when they're not.

The best resource for following these things is the internet. The internet contains lots of information on everything about computers, including the year 2000 problem. To get reserve data, look at the web site

http://www.bog.frb.fed.us/releases/

This is where the Federal Reserve posts weekly reports on bank reserves. Then you need to click on "Aggregate Reserves of Depository Institutions and the Money Base/Releases" to get the latest bi-weekly report.

Next, follow the Federal Financial Institution Examination Counsel's web site, and related links there:

The Millenium Bug Bank Panic

http://www.ffiec.gov/y2k/

They are a part of the Federal Reserve that examines banks for compliance with Federal Reserve regulations. Their site contains updates and press releases on the Year 2000 problem in the banking industry. For example, here you can learn that FFEIC is now getting involved in helping banks establish a year 2000 plan and giving them guidelines as to what constitutes a plan.

If you're not on the internet, then get on. I don't care if you're 80 years old and you've never touched a computer in your life. Get some help if you need it, but get on the net.

The Millenium Bug

10. A Short Course on National Emergencies

If the banking industry collapses, if banks close their doors and most people can't get their money out, President Clinton will declare a national emergency. Banks will be crying for help; individuals—98.8% of them—will be crying for help, and the government will step in to help. This is not merely likely. It is a dead certainty.

To understand what would happen in a national emergency caused by a banking crisis, we can only look at history—past precedents—to form a picture of how the government would handle a banking crisis in 1999. In this chapter we will look at what powers the government has legal authority to assume, as well as what powers it has assumed in the past. Then in the next chapter we will focus on the national emergency that Franklin Delano Roosevelt called in 1933 in response to a banking crisis.

The Legal Basis for Emergency Powers

Since World War I, the federal government has used the War Powers Act of 1917 as the basis for presidentially declared national emergencies. Even before World War I, there were provisions for so-called "war powers", especially in the so-called "laws of prize" on the high seas. These laws date back to the very beginning of the republic. Further precedents were set during the Civil War, in war powers assumed or given to Abraham Lincoln. The War Powers Act of 1917, however, marks the beginning of the idea of a "national emergency" that is not a war. This law was enacted at the beginning of US involvement in World War I, and it gave the President specific powers to regulate trading with the enemy:

> "That the president may investigate, regulate, or prohibit, under such rules and regulations as he may prescribe, by means of licenses or otherwise, any transactions in foreign exchange, export or earmarkings of gold or silver coin or bullion or currency, transfers of credit in any form (other than credits relating solely to transactions to be executed wholly within the United States)." *Section 5(b), the Act of October 6, 1917*

Specifically, this act applied only to "other than citizens of the United States" since citizens were understood not to be enemies. When World War I ended, however, the War Powers Act was not rescinded. It still remained in effect. In the banking crisis of 1933 Roosevelt asked Congress to modify the War Powers Act to read:

> "During time of war *or during any other period of national emergency declared by the President*, the President may, through any agency that he may designate, or otherwise, investigate, regulate, or prohibit, under such rules and regulations as he may prescribe, by means of licenses or otherwise, any transactions in foreign exchange, transfers of credit *between or payments by banking institutions as defined by the President* and export, hoarding, melting or earmarkings of gold or silver coin or bullion or currency, *by any person within the United States or anyplace subject to the jurisdiction thereof.*" (Changes italicized.)

A Short Course on National Emergencies

So citizens were now to be treated like the enemy, and this Act was no longer to apply to wartime alone, but to any presidentially declared emergency. This law is routinely cited in Executive Orders that deal with national emergencies. Congress has given blanket approval to all actions by the executive, past, present *and future*, taken under the authority of this War Powers clause:

> "The actions, regulations, rules, licenses, orders and proclamations heretofore or hereafter taken, promulgated, made, or issued by the President of the United States or the Secretary of the Treasury since March the 4th, 1933, pursuant to the authority conferred by Subsection (b) of Section 5 of the Act of October 6th, 1917, as amended, are hereby approved and confirmed."—*12 US Code, Section 95 (b)*

When Roosevelt originally took such war powers upon himself, he met opposition from the Supreme Court, who ruled that this "New Deal" was unconstitutional in *United States vs. Butler* (1935) and a number of similar cases. However, Roosevelt succeeded in stacking the court with new appointees, and in 1937 it overturned *United States vs. Butler* and upheld the broad powers Roosevelt claimed.

Since this time the courts no longer view "War Powers" as unconstitutional. Their view is that the Constitution itself makes exceptions whereby it would appear to be suspended. For example, Article 1, Section 9 states that

> "The privilege of the Writ of Habeas Corpus shall not be suspended, *unless when in cases of rebellion or invasion, the public safety may require it.*"

Thus Habeas Corpus[1] is understood as a privilege, not an inalienable right, and it may be suspended. When? In a national emergency. Similar language may be found in the 5th Amendment, which intimates that men can be held answerable for crimes without indictment or even trial during such an emergency:[2]

> No person shall be held to answer for a capital, or otherwise infamous crime, unless on a presentment or indictment of a Grand Jury, except in cases arising in the land or naval forces, or in the Militia, when in actual service in time of War or public danger...

When these Constitutional provisions, Habeas Corpus and the Fifth Amendment are abandoned, a constitutional government of laws is effectively reduced to an uncontrolled police state, which is what our federal government has essentially become today. The legal means by which this has happened is that the national emergency originally declared in 1933 has never been rescinded. That is why gold and silver were systematically removed from circulation between 1933 and 1970 even though the Constitution requires gold and silver for lawful money. That is why they have never been restored. We're still in the state of emergency. Even the U.S. Senate, in a hearing on the matter in 1973, acknowledged this fact. Our leaders haven't just somehow for-

---

1 Habeas Corpus guarantees that the government cannot hold someone without due process of law, e.g., charging them with a crime, indictment by a Grand Jury, etc.
2 An excellent treatise on this subject is Gene Schroder, *War and Emergency Powers, A Special Report on the National Emergency in the United States of America* (American Freedom Coalition, Rockwell, Texas:1995) Their phone is (972)771-1969.

gotten what the Constitution says. They've annulled it through a declaration of emergency.

These emergency provisions are no longer issued only by the executive branch. Given that the Constitution is laid aside by the presidential declaration of national emergency, Congress has gotten into the act as well, routinely enacting legislation that flies in the face of constitutional guarantees of freedom. Perhaps Congress knows that the President no longer needs their consent to legislate as he sees fit, and they go along peacefully lest they shatter the appearance that they still have some power. Thus, national emergencies have produced everything from wage and price controls to the abolition of due process in punishing the guilty by allowing various government agencies to seize property from people without even accusing them of a crime. The latest subterfuge is the war on terrorism, which is making way for any individual to have his normal rights suspended by declaring him, or an organization he belongs to "terrorist".

The Long-Term Effect of National Emergencies

The end of every national emergency, and of the state of emergency that has been in continuance since 1933, is that the government grows more powerful, claiming new rights to itself and abolishing the rights of individual citizens. In view of this fact, we must realize that neither bureaucrat nor politician is averse to a national emergency. Quite to the contrary. The national emergency is the enabling factor that allows the government—and government bureaucrats—to "get things done." The state gains more power from every emergency. New precedents are set for unilateral action.

Patrick Kennon, in his book *The Twilight of Democracy*[3], sheds some light upon why this situation has developed. His book is a discussion of the role of bureaucracy in government. He is himself a bureaucrat—a retired CIA analyst—and he believes the democratic system is ineffective and incompetent. Kennon argues this is a world of technical specialization that bureaucrats should rightly rule. This is an important book because it reveals the mindset of the bureaucrat who considers himself to be the priest of the new world order.

Kennon makes it clear in his book that large bureaucracies do not function well in so-called "normal" times. Multitudes of conflicting interests pull this way and that way at the reins of power, so that when a government agency attempts to regulate some activity, it meets resistance. Thus it cannot do its job effectively. For example, the Environmental Protection Agency is given the task of protecting the environment. It institutes all kinds of controls with that task in mind. However, economic interests continually hobble it in its work. Cities cannot afford to meet pollution standards by such-and-such a date. The logging industry just doesn't care about the plight of owls, etc., etc.

During an emergency, on the other hand, bureaucrats are handed power on a silver platter. They are given carte blanche to do whatever they "need" to do. The opposition that a bureaucracy normally faces when doing its job evaporates. To the bureaucrat, then, a national emergency becomes the key to self-realization. A great example of this was World War II. Virutally the whole

---

[3] Patrick E. Kennon, *The Twilight of Democracy* (Doubleday, New York:1995).

A Short Course on National Emergencies

economy was turned over to bureaucrats who regulated everything from how much butter you could buy to what a factory was to produce. They could even send loyal American citizens to concentration camps at a word. Opposition was unpatriotic, and bureaucrats ruled the country.

In other words, national emergencies are not, for everybody, something to be avoided. To some people they are the ticket to power, and the means by which normal opposition is short-circuited. They are the means by which politics is set aside and truly efficient government is called into action.

In the end, government according to principles is thrown out the window. Instead, we end up with a government that is driven by "public policy"—e.g. what the public wants. In such a situation, the national emergency—the crisis—is the way change is introduced. If inflation is perceived to be The Problem, then the government jumps in and does something. If drugs are The Problem, the government jumps in. If terrorism is The Problem, then guess what . . . . I hope you're getting the picture.

Why doesn't the government attend to these kinds of things long before they become crises? Why not institute sound economic policy so that inflation doesn't become a problem? Why allow millions to become addicted to drugs before doing anything? Why not have a sane foreign policy that doesn't lead half the world to hate us? The simple answer is that public support for drastic actions doesn't exist until a crisis manifests itself. So in a way, it is better to just let things go until the crisis appears. At that point, public opinion swings so decisively in favor of somebody doing something—anything—that the bureaucrats and politicians can act strongly without having to face repercussions at the ballot box.

National Emergency in the 90s

"National emergency" has become a routine way for the executive office to legislate, and indeed, control the country. Things that are in no way vital to the life of the nation are now routinely declared national emergencies. Such declarations enable the President to throw his weight around in one way or another.

Just in the past few years, President Clinton has declared national emergencies to[4]

- Prohibit development of Iranian petroleum resources.
- Implement export controls to curtail "unrestricted access of foreign parties to US goods, technology and technical data."
- Prohibit transactions with terrorists who threaten to disrupt Middle East peace processes.
- Implement export controls to retard development of nuclear, chemical and biological weapons.
- Block assets of people involved in the Bosnian-Serbian conflict
- Block assets of Hatian nationals.
- Forbid transactions with Unita in Angola.

---

4   Note that we aren't even discussing the multitudes of local emergencies which are called by governors when hurricanes, earthquakes, or floods strike, or riots start. These also invoke reams of emergency regulations and get the Federal Emergency Management Administration involved, with its own set of federal regulations.

A Short Course on National Emergencies 95

These national emergencies have been declared using wording describing how such problems constitute "unusual and extraordinary threats to national security, foreign policy and the economy of the US." With the possible exception of nuclear, chemical and biological weapon development it is difficult to see how these things really constitute national emergencies—or for that matter to believe that they even really concern us. Yet the law says that there is a national emergency whenever the President declares one. It is left entirely at his discretion.

In essence, the national emergency has become a normal part of American life. While the concept of a real "emergency" is lost in this game, the very broad powers delegated to the President in time of national emergency have not likewise been diluted. The original War Powers Act of 1917 still stands, giving the President virtually unlimited power over the economy. Furthermore, the president can clarify or expand these powers at will by issuing more executive orders. Executive Order 12919, released by President Clinton on June 6, 1994, spells out some of the powers that the President assumes under a national emergency. In it, he assumes the power to control all transportation, "regardless of ownership", all forms of energy, all farm equipment, all fertilizer, all food resources, all food resource facilities, all health resources, all metals and minerals and all water resources. Add to this other executive orders of historical significance such as 10995, which provides for the seizure of all communications media in the United States, or 11002, empowering the Postmaster General to register every person in the US, or 11000, which provides for uncompensated work forces under federal supervision, even breaking up families, and the President has virtually absolute power over everything you own and do. If it isn't on the books right now, there is a precedent for it in past executive orders or legislation, and more can be written at will.

Neither is the year 2000 problem beyond the purview of the executive office. On February 4, 1998, President Clinton issued the first executive order dealing with the millenium bug.[5] All it does is create a new "Council on Year 2000 Conversion" and declare that the government cannot tolerate disruptions in critical federal programs, asserting authority over not only federal systems, but state and local, as well as "private sector operations of critical national and local systems, including the banking and finanical system." While this E.O. may seem benign on a first reading, it clearly reveals that the President is moving in the direction of viewing the bug as a national emergency.

Now, with that in mind, let's go on and look at how a previous banking crisis was handled, and how it could parallel a banking crisis in 1999 . . . .

---

5 This executive order is so new at this writing that it doesn't even have a number yet. You can, however, view it and other E.O.'s issued by President Clinton at *www.whitehouse.gov*.

11. 1933 and 1999: A Comparison

To understand how a banking crisis surrounding the millenium bug would play itself out, it is essential to understand that the real crisis will occur *before* the millenium turns over, maybe in the last few months of 1999, but maybe as early as 1998. That is when the bank runs would take place—as people are preparing for the change of the millenium. That is when interest rates would go sky high. (In the last edition of this book, I didn't expect runs would take place until late 1999, but I wouldn't bet on that now. The key is when media publicity reaches critical mass, and it seems to be moving much more quickly than I thought six months ago.)

Because the millenium will not have turned over yet, computers will still be functioning. Only software that is looking a few months in advance will face potential problems. The rest of it will be humming along.

This is an essential fact. If a banking crisis were to begin on January 1, 2000 or later, then it would only be a part of a multi-faceted emergency that would involve a hobbled government that was trying to get its computers working properly to start with. However, if the banking crisis starts in 1999, it will not be compounded by other events. The computers will still be running when the crisis hits. The government will still be running too.

As such, the government will still be competent to respond to the crisis, and it will respond to it as a financial emergency, rather than a general emergency. This emergency may broaden in scope as January 1, 2000 approaches; however, either legislation or executive orders will already have been put in place by then to deal with the existing emergency.

Let there be no doubt that a banking crisis as a result of people anticipating the millenium bug would certainly be considered a national emergency. If bank runs develop by the end of the millenium, only 1.2% of depositors will get their money out. Then the banks will close their doors. This will leave 98.8% of the people without access to their funds. They won't be able to pay their electric bill or their rent. They won't be able to buy groceries. These 98.8% will consider the situation to be a national emergency. They will be screaming for help from anyone who can give it, and they will take help in any form it comes. Much lighter troubles have caused the public to request national emergency powers be given to the president in this decade. During the UPS strike in the summer of 1997, many businesses were asking the president to declare a national emergency and send the drivers back to work. That is an utter triviality compared to what will happen when banks start closing. If the American public can't abide a UPS strike, they'll squeal like hogs being slaughtered when the banks close.

Since the first national emergency associated with the millenium changeover will be financial, we can learn a lot about what to expect by looking at the only other "national emergency" of a financial character in America's history, the one declared in March, 1933 by President Franklin Delano Roosevelt.

In 1933 the deflationary cycle of the previous few years was forcing people to eat into savings. Banks were

1933 and 1999: A Comparison

closing as a result, and people were losing their money. On March 2, the Federal Reserve Bank of New York advised President Hoover to declare a national emergency due to "continued and increasing withdrawal of currency and gold from the banks of the country." Hoover did not comply, however Franklin D. Roosevelt, inaugurated on March 4, 1933, did. He declared a national emergency and called Congress into session. He declared a banking holiday, and asked Congress to authorize a new emergency currency, Federal Reserve Bank Notes, while authorizing the Secretary of the Treasury to require all "gold coin, gold bullion and gold certificates" to be surrendered. In effect, Roosevelt transformed the US monetary system overnight.

By and large, being able to get one's money out of the bank to pay bills and feed the family was a whole lot more important than some constitutional technicality. Unbacked paper that people would accept as money was better than nothing at all. So the change was accepted. That is understandable enough.

Yet Roosevelt's plan for changing the currency was diabolically seductive. It obviously wasn't something that was cooked up on the first evening he was in office. Let's consider it:

First, Roosevelt outlawed ownership of gold, except for coins with numismatic value and jewelry.

By outlawing the ownership of gold, Roosevelt brought even those who had escaped the banking collapse back into the system. Talking to people who lived through this demonetization, there appeared to be a lot of confusion about what gold had to be turned in. The public announcement stated that "*all* gold coin, gold bullion and gold certificates" had to be turned in, but vaguely noted "exceptions allowed" which included numismatic coins and jewelry. Gold had to be turned in by May 1, 1933 with the threat of 10 years or $10,000 fine for failure to do so. Of course, the most powerful and influential people—the people who had gold—got it out of the country. Others simply held on to gold coins and jewelry to the extent that they dared to. So Roosevelt was shrewd enough to reward those who had escaped from the government's maw—who had refused to turn in their gold at $20/ounce—to come back. The official price of gold was set at $35/ounce in January, 1934—considerably higher than the approximately $20/ounce before the demonetization. Thus, people who brought their assets back to the US, exchanging their gold for dollars at $35/ounce were paid a tidy profit of 75%.[2] This was a strong enticement at the time—in the middle of an all-out depression when money was hard to come by.

Second, Roosevelt outlawed contracts payable in gold.

Outlawing gold-based contracts essentially killed gold as a medium of exchange. It meant that every contract, including the paper money which promised to pay in gold coin, including the bank deposit of gold coin, was no longer to be paid in gold, but in paper. In essence, any gold you had loaned out, or earned but not collected, was confiscated and replaced with paper. Stopping the coinage of gold and replacing it with currency only reinforced killing gold-based contracts. Gold would no longer be available as an option to the general public.

The outlawing of gold clauses in contracts was also a cunning play upon people's greed. After all, if you had

---

[2] The average law-abiding citizen, of course, had already turned his gold in before the revaluation, so he didn't get to cash in on this bonanza.

1933 and 1999: A Comparison

a contract with someone to pay them so many dollars in gold coin (at $20/ounce) and you had official sanction to pay them in paper dollars (effectively paying them 75% less), it would be altogether too easy to renege on the agreement to pay in gold. What a boon to anybody who owed money!

Think about this: a nation that was probably 90% or better Christian took Jesus' command to let your "yes" be yes and your "no" be no and threw it out the window because the government asked them to and gave them permission to do so. After all, just because the government would no longer enforce a clause in a contract to pay in gold coin, does that somehow invalidate the contract? Does that let a man off of keeping his word before God? No. And yet a whole nation decided they would renege on their contracts. At heart, they did it because they could get away with it. The courts wouldn't uphold this aspect of such contracts. So, happy with the fact that their debts were effectively reduced by 75%, they partnered with their government in defrauding one another.

Thus, the government handled the "national emergency" of 1933 not just by forcing everyone to accept a system of fiat money. Rather, force was coupled with seductive enticements to cooperate—75% profits on gold, and an effective 75% reduction of debts. This was nothing less than playing upon sin in the hearts of men.

And since the national emergency was never cancelled, the changes made in 1933 were, for all intents and purposes, permanent and irrevocable. They only made way for further changes down the road. At first US currency was redeemable for gold overseas at the $35/ounce rate, and silver coin still circulated freely in the US. In 1965 silver coin was replaced with base metal.

Then the gold backing of the dollar was removed in 1971, when it had become a mere formality to US citizens. *Understand that Roosevelt's handling of the national emergency will be a model for the banking emergency in 1999.*

What happens in 1999 may be floated as temporary provisions, but the changes made will permanently change the way the banking system works from that point onward. Just as gold has never returned, so too, the changes we will experience will be irreversible once in place.

What will these changes entail?

While it is difficult to prognosticate about future events, this national emergency could conceivably be the event that ushers in an all-electronic money system. Basically, when the government is faced with a situation where people want to get out of "the system" but can't, it can do one of three things:

1) Stand back and let the 1.2% who got out remain safe, and the 98.8% who didn't suffer,

2) Provide a means for everyone who so desires to get out, or

3) Close off the escape hatch so that no one can escape from the system, whether he wants to or not.

We can be certain that the government will not stand back when 98.8% of the people are demanding action. No way. This leaves only options 2 or 3 open. Basically, option 2 involves printing lots of money, and option 3 involves moving into an all-electronic money system.

There are a number of reasons why printing lots of money is not a viable solution in government eyes.

1933 and 1999: A Comparison

Most importantly, cash is untraceable for tax purposes and for purposes of control. To take a large part of the money supply and turn it into cash would make a large part of the economy untraceable.

A government that is starved for revenues is naturally intent on bleeding everyone for as much as it can. Untraceable cash transactions open the door to unreported income and unpaid taxes, unlicensed business operations, and so on. That's why there has been a steady war on cash, which has included instituting reporting requirements for cash transactions of $10,000 or more, the routine seizure of cash in police investigations, increased IRS scrutiny, the printing of new money, the retirement of large bills ($500 and up) and more.

To release a large amount of cash into the system—especially at a time when people might just think the IRS will be ineffective anyhow—would mean more untraceable transactions, more unpaid taxes, and less overall control.

Next, it is not physically possible for the Bureau of Engraving and Printing to print enough paper money to significantly expand the money supply. The BEP prints about 9 billion notes a year, and they are running at full capacity already. Presses run 24 hours a day already. To print $1 trillion in $100 bills would mean an additional 10 billion notes. That would cover about 1/4 of the money supply, but it is impossible. New printing presses—very special equipment—have to be ordered years in advance. New plants are not built overnight.[3]

---

3 Franklin Sanders, *The Moneychanger*, December, 1997, January, 1998.

The other option would be to issue a low quality currency, printed on offset presses. The problem is, such currency is trivial to counterfeit in today's world of scanners, laser printers and photocopiers. Although sufficient volume of currency might be produced this way, it could—and would—be counterfeited literally within hours of issuance. Any high-tech counterfeiting deterrent would require time to invent and test. Given the government's usual agility in making decisions and inventing solutions to problems, we can rule out a low quality, easy to produce currency that won't be counterfeited the minute it's released.

Then there is the problem of the effect of all this new cash on the economy. Because of reserve ratios, every $100 in new deposits would multiply into $5819.32 (at current reserve ratios). Given an easy out from the system, only those who saw the millenium bug as a real problem would get out. Those who stayed in would collect cash from those who got out as goods and services were traded. They would then deposit the money in the bank and fuel the fractional reserve system. Considering that the people who fear the millenium bug and the people who do not could be changing places from day to day, one would suspect that printing money would lead to gross instability in the money supply. One day, banks could be closing and the next day they could be flooded with deposits and multiplying the money supply out of this world. This would cause inflation to kick in with a vengeance.

Even worse, if there were any question that the cash might end up being worthless after the millenium due to a computer-induced government default, or because an emergency, low-quality note would be recalled, then people would bid up the price of goods and services all

1933 and 1999: A Comparison

the more in an attempt to spend the money before it becomes worthless.

Inflation is, at present, something that our federal government must avoid at all costs. When inflation kicks in again, it will sink the whole system and totally rearrange the political landscape. Such is the politics of debt, which we'll discuss in a few pages.

For now, understand that releasing a large amount of cash into the system to resolve bank runs will generate tremendous instability in an economy that is changing from day to day as the result of a short-term technical problem.

Finally, feeding a panic tends to cause it to grow. To start printing paper money in order to help people get out of the banking system before the technical year 2000 problem is realized is tantamount to admitting the banking system really does have a problem, and the average citizen had better get out while he can. It is official encouragement to get out while the getting is good.

All of these factors make issuing lots of paper money to resolve a banking crisis problematic at best. Obviously, they also provide convenient excuses for those who do not wish to increase the role of cash in the economy, but to decrease it.

Already, the War Powers Act of 1917 provides for a very different solution: keeping people locked inside the system whether they like it or not. Remember that War Powers give the President power to control foreign exchange, as well as the export or hoarding of gold, silver *or currency?* In other words, he has complete control over the entire monetary system, provided he simply declares a national emergency.

1933 is a model for how to close off the escape hatch so that people will be trapped in the system. In 1933, the escape hatch was gold coin. It was the real money, and everything else amounted to promises to pay (in gold).

People who want to get out of the banking system in 1999 will largely seek to convert their bank deposits into currency. Although some will seek to convert their currency into gold, the expense of buying gold and then selling it again after the millenium change will run at least 10% of the amount converted. Compare this to currency, where the only expense will be the interest lost on the bank deposit, less taxes. As such, gold will be viewed by the majority of people as a much more expensive form of insurance than currency. Currency, and not gold, will be the insurance of choice.

However, just as the banking problems of 1933 were resolved by forcing people to stop using gold, so the banking crisis of 1999—if one develops—will very likely be resolved by forcing people to stop using currency.

Think about this with me for a moment:

- All of the fear associated with the millenium bug will center around the electronic system. There may be only a small percentage of people who truly fear the problems the bug could cause, but this small percentage is capable of collapsing the whole highly leveraged system.

- In 1999—the most likely time for a crisis—the computers will still be running smoothly. Thus an effective, coordinated response by both government and the financial community will still be possible.

- All the prognostications of electronic doom will be at best educated guesses at this time, whereas the banking crisis will be very real. Such doom-sayers could be blamed for exaggerating the problem and causing the

1933 and 1999: A Comparison

collapse, and possibly even labeled terrorists and shut up.

- A vast majority of the people will demand an immediate answer to the banking problem. They won't be able to wait even a couple of weeks to see how the millenium bug pans out.

In such an environment, it would be easy to call those people who have taken their money out of the bank "currency hoarders," especially if the millenium bug is played down by government officials. This is something that the president can regulate under the amended War Powers Act of 1917. Remember, it specifically covers "export, hoarding, melting or earmarking of gold or silver coin or bullion or currency."

To declare a national emergency because of a banking crisis has a precedent in history.

To use emergency powers to stop the hoarding of currency has a precedent in history.

"Currency hoarding" can easily be curtailed with a Roosevelt-style program of making currency no-longer-negotiable. In other words, just as Roosevelt took our economy into a fiat currency-based system, so President Clinton could take our economy into an electronic currency-based system.

Of course, there are some important differences between 1999 and 1933. In 1933, gold had intrinsic value and it was easy to hide. That meant coercion would not be effective to force people to surrender their gold. They would simply hide it. Some reward for surrendering it was necessary. Thus Roosevelt combined rewards with punishments. He rewarded people who had gold with a

75% profit. This took gold out of circulation overnight. (Bad money always drives out good.) He forbade the use of gold in commerce by revoking the gold clause in contracts, rewarding debtors who chose not to honor their contracts.

In 1999, currency has no intrinsic value. Although it can be hidden just as easily as gold, it can also be demonetized and made worthless at the stroke of a pen. As such, offering people a reward to surrender currency may not be necessary. The number of people who hold any significant amount of currency will be small and politically impotent. The political backlash for simply demonetizing it after such-and-such a date may be nil. "Currency hoarders" can be offered amnesty for a short period of time to turn in their currency and join the system again. Those who do not will simply watch their "money" lose all value. For all the rest of the people who get caught in bank runs, the choice will be merely one of whether they will be able to use the money they have caught in the system or not, and of course these people would rather use it.[4]

There are a few considerations against a complete, forced demonetization of currency. Some of these take the form of resistance by the people, which could materialize. We'll discuss resistance later in this book. However there are also practical considerations. One is the fact that US currency is used as a medium of exchange

---

4 The one exception to this is the few people who own gold and silver. Gold may well be outlawed again, perhaps right along with silver. However, since it has intrinsic value, the government will have to offer some enticement to get people to turn it in if they seriously expect them to do so.

throughout the world. Another is the need for small change in vending machines, etc.

As such, the demonetization of currency may come in stages, just as the demonetization of gold and silver. Just as small silver coins continued to circulate for years, change may continue to circulate for use in vending machines. Likewise, paper currency may remain negotiable abroad, at least in limited quantities. Although most of the first world nations may go with an electronic money system which could be integrated across borders,[5] third world nations generally do not have the resources for such things, and may not for 50 years. As such, the currency could not be eliminated entirely without causing severe dislocations in foreign relations. Some accomodation to this fact will be necessary, just like US currency was redeemable in gold for foreigners for nearly 40 years.

In summary, the millenium bug could prove to be the ultimate opportunity for those who already wish to create an all-electronic monetary system. Handled shrewdly, the transition to such a system could be made almost overnight, with very little opposition.

---

5 The European economic union is essentially driving most of Europe toward an electronic system already.

The Millenium Bug

12. Who Wants an Electronic Money System?

In addressing the question of who wants this electronic money system, we must enter a world of smoke and mirrors. Speculation concerning who is behind the drive toward electronic money is rampant, and definitive statements by powerful people are practically non-existent.

Over the years, various authors have claimed that there are real conspirators behind ideas like a one-world electronic money system. The Bilderbergers, the Trilateral Commission, the Council on Foreign Relations, and like organizations come to mind. They are quiet about what they're doing, and they have enough financial and political clout to be a threat. It is all too easy to blame such groups for trends we see in society that we don't like.

One can understand these secret societies easily enough in simple terms. Most people want to protect their assets and improve their economic position, and most of us are not above manipulating politicians to do it. We will cast our votes against a politician who says he's going to raise taxes, for example. We will write a letter to Congress complaining about some new bill that would adversely affect our bottom line, or encourage a vote for a bill that would help us out. We'll get scared over some proposal that will end up getting us all nuked.

Now, imagine your net worth is $100 billion instead of $100,000. Of course you're going to want to protect it. You don't want a bunch of doltish politicians coming up with some half-baked idea that will make them popular at the polls while robbing you blind. So you'll do what you can to keep them from doing such things. If that means buying them, manipulating them, or coercing them, you'll do it. So maybe groups like the Trilateral Commission aren't as demonic as the ordinary man sometimes thinks. At least, no more demonic than the ordinary man himself! (And of course, a cashless society in the hands of bankers would be of benefit to the bankers.)

Regardless of the conspiracy theories, the cashless society is coming. It won't require a conspiracy to bring it about. It needn't have anything to do with world government, secret societies, or banking cartels. It needn't have anything to do with the mark of the beast in Revelation. Adding conspiracies to the equation may make these things happen faster, or it may direct the final form they take, but they are unnecessary elements in the equation. Simple questions of economics and control are enough to bring us a cashless society shortly no matter what.

To properly see what is likely to happen in the next couple years, it's really best to jettison some of the common ideas about a cashless society that are floating around now. Too often, they are so wrapped up in conspiracy theories or end times theology that they miss the simplicity of it. When I say "cashless society", if you think of a super-computerized society, where everyone is tracked, where you have a chip implant, or a bar code, and every store has a scanner to read your hand, you're

Who Wants an Electronic Money System? 113

missing the point completely. While such things may come in time, all I'm really talking about in the transition period is moving to a system in which there is no paper money circulating. Rather than requiring *more* computing power—something that would be difficult at a time when computers are going down—it would require *less* computing power. In a sense, it would be a *simplification* of our present economy, because all of the accounting and accounting software required to keep track of cash could be done away with. Perhaps the accounting required to keep track of paper checks could be done away with too. At a time when businesses will have to be deciding what parts of their computer systems to salvage and what parts to allow to go down, any simplification that is possible will be not just welcome, it will be downright necessary.

With that in mind, let's take a look at how we're already 90% of the way to a cashless society as it is.

Checks and Electronic Money

While we are not used to thinking of a paper check as electronic money, the truth is, it really is. Writing a check and cashing it in today's world does not cause paper money or gold to be transferred from one bank or another, or anything like that. It migh have caused such a physical transfer in 1860 or 1940, but not anymore. A check is now nothing more than a written order for your bank to transfer electronic funds to the bank of whomever you wrote the check to.

Basically, your bank takes the checks you deposit and every other check it receives, adds them up, and submits them to the Federal Reserve system for processing each day. They also receive from the Federal Reserve every check written by their customers. The difference between what they submit and what they get back is credited or debited to their account, and they accordingly credit or debit your account. No paper money changes hands. It's all electronic.

Once we realize that even paper checks are part of an electronic money system, albeit a rather antiquated and cumbersome part of it, it should be clear that we are very close to a cashless society already. Much of the drive toward a more obviously electronic system centers around getting rid of the relic of paper checks.

The Automated Checking Account

Banks are increasingly attempting to attract new customers with low cost services. The ten million federal benefit recipients who don't have bank accounts are just one example of people who could honestly use banking services. These people might not maintain balances significant enough to justify giving them a free account, yet they find the cost of an ordinary checking account an unnecessary expense.

Banks are using computer technology to reduce the costs of maintaining basic accounts so they can attract customers from these groups. For example, Bank of America offers the Versateller checking account, which is free of cost and has no minimum balance. This account gives the customer free deposits and withdrawals, provided they are done through the Automated Teller (called Versateller). If the customer wants to make a transaction by going to the teller in the bank, he must pay a $1.25 fee per transaction. Thus automated teller machines, which are nothing more than computers, open up new services which save money for both banks and their customers. Some banks are beginning to offer services

Who Wants an Electronic Money System? 115

via the internet, or via modem dial-ups, so their more sophisticated customers don't even have to leave home in order to do their banking. For the less computer-saavy, banking by phone is a booming business.

Likewise, some banks offer businesses reduced rates on electronic payments. For example, the bank might charge 12 cents to process a check from the account, and 26 cents for a deposit but allow an unlimited number of free electronic credits and debits. This encourages businesses to use electronic payment systems by passing on the cost savings that banks realize with electronic payments.

Credit, Debit and Smart Cards

The use of credit cards and debit cards to make routine transactions is growing by leaps and bounds. Visa, for example, has nearly 600 million cards in circulation. Mastercard has some 400 million, and they are growing at a rate of about 22% per year. Both companies are aggressively pursuing the development of smart cards that will allow consumers to access bank accounts and account information, access credit accounts, and even store cash electronically.

Development of the smart cash card is following similar lines to the development of the credit card. Back in the 1960's, various merchants began offering credit cards to their clients. These revolving charge cards were only good with the merchant who issued them, but they proved a boon to companies like Sears, J.C. Penny, and gasoline companies. The universal credit card—MasterCard, Visa, American Express, Discover, etc.—developed quite naturally from the success of the merchant-issued card. At first the cards were only regional, then national, and now worldwide.

Credit cards are widely used not just because they allow people to spend money before they get it, but because they allow the user to reduce paperwork. One can buy 50 different things in a month and receive one itemized statement explaining exactly how much was spent and where. One can then pay for it all with a single check, instead of fifty of them. This alone saves time and money. Going even further, some credit cards, such as Discover, have offered cardholders a cash-back incentive to use the card. Typically, the cardholder will get 1% back on all his purchases in a year. That can add up to a significant amount of money, which is a big incentive to use the card.

In the same way, cash cards have become increasingly popular in the past few years. Bus and subway cards have been quite popular for over a decade. The latest fad is pre-paid phone cards, which allow people to buy $10 or so of long distance service at a time, and use it wherever they are. There is no longer a need to get a pocket full of change to phone home from a pay phone. You can pick up a card at any grocery store or convenience store, or even the local post office.

The universal cash card seems to be an obvious, logical follow-on to the dedicated-use cash card issued by some merchants. With this universal cash card, one would be able to make a long distance call, ride the bus, or buy a candy bar from a vending machine. These cards might be sold in supermarkets too, and be either rechargeable or for one-time use.

The Cashless Government

By January 1, 1999, the US government will make all payments electronically. These include social security and disability payments, and payments for goods and

Who Wants an Electronic Money System? 117

services. Already, as of June 26, 1996, all new benefits recipients must receive payments directly into their bank accounts, or they can't get paid. By 1999, the system will, by law, include everyone receiving benefits, even the 10 million or so recipients who do not have bank accounts at this time. This move toward a cashless government was mandated by the Electronic Funds Transfer Expansion Act of 1996.

Under the Electronic Benefits Transfer Program, part of the Welfare Reform Act of 1996, food stamps and government welfare benefits will be distributed by way of a government-issued debit card, starting no later than October 1, 2002. These programs are administered by the states, so states are in charge of implementation. Some states, such as Maryland, have already implemented such a program.

Again, the IRS has mandated electronic fund transfers for payments of withholding taxes by employers. The current requirement is that all employers with $50,000 annual tax payments or more must pay electronically. On January 1, 1999, this threshold will go down to $20,000, and eventually to zero.

Is this conditioning for the New World Order? Maybe, but if we look under the hood at the engine that is driving these changes, it boils down to money. During the first half of fiscal year 1997, the US Treasury made 424 million payments, 58% of which were electronic. A check costs the government 43 cents to issue, versus two cents for an electronic transfer. That adds up to a nice $174 million in savings. Double it for a year: $348 million. Add to this $100 million in postage, handling 1.7 million inquiries about lost checks, and 100,000 incidents of fraud due to mail theft, forgery and counterfeiting.[1] It's quite a chunk of money! Going electronic just makes good business sense. It saves taxpayers money—at least a half billion a year, or $2 for every man, woman and child in the US.

Maryland's state benefit system distributes $59 million monthly, and will save $750,000 per year in its new electronic form.[2] Food stamp recipients also gave the system an 83% favorable rating. They didn't have to pick up their food stamps, they didn't have to worry about somebody stealing them, and they didn't have the embarrassment of paying with food stamps. In other words, everyone seems to agree it's better and easier.

The US government alone accounts for about one fifth of the entire gross domestic product. Their decision to go electronic means nothing less than the full implementation of a major electronic payment system before 1999 and the conversion of a huge part of the economy over to electronics.

Time and Money

In the end, it is time and money that are driving the increasing use of electronic payments. In a hectic world, time is valuable. If you can save people time with some new device, you have something marketable. Likewise, nobody will ever complain about saving money.

So to answer the question, "Who wants an electronic money system?" The answer is, just about everybody, in one form or another. In an ideal world, this would be the end of the matter. In a world of computers, electronic money is superior to trinket-like coins and paper, and it is superior to paper checks.

---

1 Bill Orr, "Uncle Sam Goes Digital", *ABA Banking Journal Online*, July, 1997.
2 *Ibid.*, p.4.

Who Wants an Electronic Money System?

Of course, ours is far from an ideal world. It's only when we start to consider the fact that a lot of people—and especially the government—will do just about anything to get their hands on your money that complications arise.

Crime and Control

Crime is a growing problem around the world. Criminals are always finding new ways to use an increasingly technological system, and technological advances are making new crimes possible that no one had ever thought of before. For example, the immense drug trade that has grown up in the last half of the twentieth century is largely possible because of airplanes. The idea of carting loads of cocaine from Columbia to the United States on burros would have been ridiculous a century ago.

New crimes are emerging all the time. For example, it's recently been reported that a criminal ring is abducting business fliers at airports, taking them to local hotels, harvesting their kidneys, and leaving them with instruction how to keep alive until emergency personnel can rush them to the hospital. Their kidneys are sold for a handsome sum on the black market. What next?

Technology always creates new opportunities for criminals. And the guardians of society naturally use technology to stay a step ahead of the criminals. But it is a vicious cycle.

We have to understand the drive toward electronic money itself as part of this cycle. Law enforcement agencies would like to have an all-electronic money system purely as a way to combat crime. They could clean up the drug trade, because people couldn't conduct anonymous transactions anymore. They could shut down the underground economy, and bring in additional tax revenues. They could investigate crimes more readily, and perhaps even anticipate crimes. For example, if a certain individual went and bought the ingredients for some plastic explosive at several different chemical supply houses, he could be spotted on a computer that checks for such things, and interrogated before he even had a chance to commit a crime.

That law enforcement is interested in such capabilities is plain from the financial monitoring that has already been implemented. Most notorious is the monitoring that the IRS does of our annual tax returns. They collect information from a variety of sources about our income. If what we say on the tax return doesn't match up with what those other sources report, we'll have some explaining to do. Likewise, the 1970 Banking Secrecy Act requires all US banks to collect detailed data on their customers and make it available on request to law enforcement agencies. Credit card transactions are subject to the same reporting. Again, the US Treasury Department has set up FINCEN, the Financial Crimes Enforcement Network, a giant computer that uses artificial intelligence to cross-reference several databases of financial information about every person in the United States. With this data, they build financial profiles, looking for so-called financial crimes, like money laundering and tax evasion.

Monitoring goes beyond the financial realm too. In 1994 our Congress gave us a new law that requires the phone company to install the electronic capability for the government to monitor up to 10% of all phone calls at any given time.[3] New bills are always in the works, too.

---

3 The Communications Assistance for Law Enforcement Act of

Who Wants an Electronic Money System?

These already-implemented programs make it very plain that law enforcement is interested in the capabilities of computers to analyze financial transactions to root out crime. A universal electronic money system would make that job ever so much easier.

Unfortunately, in democratic systems, crime often becomes an excuse for control. *Anything* can be defined as a federal crime as long as half of Congress wants it to be, and the President approves. The more crimes a country creates, the more criminals it will have, and the more criminals it has, the more controls and protections will be necessary.

At the same time, we must understand that this isn't purely an "us-versus-them" game, unless "we" are the criminal element. After all, many of the crimes that law enforcement could prevent would be attacks on innocent individuals. Though few of us may have much sympathy with the IRS collecting more taxes, who wouldn't be happy with the idea that an electronic money system will prevent their kidneys being harvested against their will and sold on the black market?

Funding the Government

Another reason for interest in an electronic money system is the continued funding of the government. When government casts off fiscal restraint in order to grow without limit, the "standard" means for funding it break down from time to time, and those standard means have to be replaced with something else. Right now, government is funded by a combination of taxes and debt. The amount of debt that any government can float

---

1994, popularly known as the "Wiretap Bill".

has limits, though. We are reaching those limits. Already Japan has threatened to dump US securities and buy gold, while quietly moving into the gold market.[4] Debt will soon cease to be a viable way to finance the government. Something else will be necessary. This "something else" will be greatly facilitated by an electronic money system, because the cashless society will make controlling people, production, taxes, and the economy easier.

This need for new methods of funding government is a very important aspect of the forces driving us toward an electronic money system. I don't want to brush it aside with a few terse comments. As such, we will examine it more thoroughly in the next two chapters. If we can see how the present system is breaking down, and how the millenium bug will likely push it over the edge, we will better understand the shape of things to come.

---

4 Michael J. Kosares, "The Real Story Behnind Central Bank Gold Sales", *Money World*, November, 1997, p. 22.

13. The Politics of Debt

When an economy undergoes a long period of prosperity, people naturally tend to become dependent on the prosperity. They forget the bad times and assume that things will only continue as-is or get better. They conduct their lives and their financial affairs in such a way that they become increasingly dependent on the good times to continue. Not only do they become dependent on the good times to continue, they also do things that will artificially extend the good times.

These actions and dependencies revolve chiefly around *credit*.

Economies tend to work in a cyclical fashion. Most likely, this is because people don't learn lessons from history, and they don't listen to their elders. As such, they tend to repeat the mistakes of the past, and reap the same consequences of those mistakes again and again and again, generation after generation. People motivated by greed tend to grasp harder and harder for more and more in the good times. They use credit to do it. They take bigger and bigger risks to achieve their goals. Then, when the tide turns, their house of cards comes crashing down. This is a phenomenon that has played itself out again and again over the centuries.

Right now, we are nearing the end of one of these credit cycles. It is a cycle that has caught up just about everybody in our society: individuals, investors, businesses and government.

At the end of a credit cycle, an economy tends to become very fragile—more vulnerable to any kind of bad news. That is true simply because people who are betting a lot on continued prosperity are likely to lose a lot when that prosperity doesn't continue.

Understand that all debt (credit) is essentially a bet on the future. The debtor is—consciously or unconsciously—betting that things will go well enough in his future that he'll be able to repay his debts, plus interest. Individuals take out mortgages and car loans, or run up their credit cards in the belief that their jobs will be sufficient to pay the bills when they come due. Companies take out loans, believing that they will be able to pay them back with future earnings. Lenders lend in the belief that the borrowers they lend to will be able to pay them back.

In the United States today, debt has risen to record levels. Let's consider a few figures: The average American household is $71,500 in debt.[1] That household spends an average 20% of its income servicing its debt. Public (e.g. government) debt is approaching $6 trillion, with unfunded liabilities, such as Social Security, Medicare, and pension fund guarantees $13 trillion.[2] Fourteen percent of the US budget is interest on the national debt. Commercial debt is about $11 trillion.[3] However you

---

1 Including mortgage debt
2 This figure can vary widely, depending on what is included. Here we are only considering retirement guarantees, and not the multitudes of mortgages, bank deposits, student loans, etc., that are guaranteed by the government.
3 Non-federal debt as reported by Federal Reserve money

The Politics of Debt

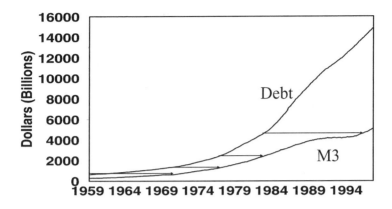

Fig. 1: Growing debt demands a growing money supply.

measure it, debt is at record levels—the highest it has ever been in our history.

As people continue to bet on the future by running up their debts, the bet becomes ever more dangerous. The economy becomes more and more dependent on interest rates to stay low, or even go down. Individuals, businesses, and government all run up their debts to the maximum level that their incomes will service. If incomes fall or interest rates increase, things will get tough.

These dangers are translated into powerful political pressures to keep interest rates low and keep the economy humming along.

Traditionally, the means we have used to cover debt is inflation of the money supply. Let's look at some numbers to see how this works: In January, 1959 the broadest measure of the money supply, M3, stood at

---

supply reports.

$292 billion. At the same time, debt (commercial paper) was reported at $641.9 billion (See Fig. 1). In other words, there was $349.9 billion in debt that could not be covered by the money supply. That debt effectively necessitated an increase in the money supply. It had to be paid, somehow. That $641.9 billion in debt in 1959 was effectively a bet by both borrowers and lenders that when the time came for it to be paid, there would be $641.9 billion available to pay it in the future when it came due. Well guess what? Come August, 1970, M3 reached $643.6 billion. In other words, *in a space of about 11 years, the money had become available to pay the debt.* The money supply had been inflated. Of course, in August, 1970 the debt had ballooned to $1.376 trillion. More new debts had been incurred than old ones had been paid down. This cycle repeated itself again in seven years. By May, 1977 the money supply, M3, had reached $1.371 trillion. Enough to cover 1970's debts . . . but the debt had reached $2.606 trillion. Six years later—1983— we'd gone through another cycle, with M3 at $2.614 trillion and debt at $5.161 trillion. After that, it took fourteen years to complete the next cycle. In July, 1997 M3 was $5.139 trillion and debt was at $14.891 trillion.

This is obviously a simplified analysis of the situation. The Federal Reserve's debt figures don't include all the debt by any means, and trying to pay the debt down with M3 would implode the whole banking system. However I hope you get the idea of what is going on here. The money supply has been systematically inflated to pay the debt.

Now consider the ratio of debt to M3. (Figure 2) Historically, it has hovered around 2. Even during the severe inflation years of the late seventies when debt was very costly due to high rates, it only went down to about 1.9. In the mid 90's, this ratio went up over 3. Common

The Politics of Debt

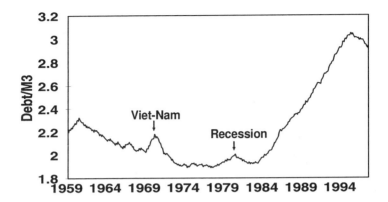

Fig. 2: Ratio of debt to money supply (M3).

sense would thus suggest that M3 will have to nearly triple in the next ten years, plus or minus a few years. Otherwise there is just too much debt and not enough money to pay it, so defaults will skyrocket.

Something is going to have to give. Debt is at record highs. The money supply to pay that debt doesn't exist. Everybody—individuals, corporations and government—is dependent on relatively low interest rates to make their payments. If debt continues to grow but the money supply does not, rates will have to go up as demand outstrips supply.

The problem is, sooner or later we're going to have to face the reality of our debts and cover them, either by paying them or defaulting on them. In the end, one of four things must always happen with debt:

1) Debt will be paid off
2) Debt will be defaulted upon
3) The money supply must be inflated
4) Interest rates will increase dramatically

In the absence of paydown or outright default, debt must continue to grow without limit. All debts accrue interest and so, if they're not paid down, they naturally grow bigger and bigger. If the money supply doesn't grow fast enough to cover debts, the cost of capital will eventually go up, as more and more people compete for the same pool of funds, and lenders cover growing losses.

Add to this the fact that our society's debts simply *cannot* be paid off. Given the current money supply—even the broadest measure of it—there simply isn't enough money available to do it. It is a mathematical impossibility, given the current money supply. The only alternatives left are (2) and (3) above. The only ways to cover today's debts are outright default or inflation.

Taking a closer look, defaults have already been skyrocketing. There were 1.1 million bankruptcies in 1996. Credit card defaults added up to more than 4% of all credit card debt last year.[4] Also notice that little downturn at the very end of the graph in Figure 2. What this tells us is that, even though debt has been growing exponentially, the money supply is now being expanded even faster. In other words, the government definitely is monetizing the debt. Wage and price inflation hasn't kicked in yet, but it will if the money supply continues to expand.

The situation we're in right now is a tough predicament for the U.S. government and the Federal Reserve. The political impetus to keep the economy humming is tremendous. It has put presidents in office and ruined

---

4 "Credit Card Delinquencies Reach 10-year High", *USA Today*, September 11, 1997.

The Politics of Debt

political careers. It has permitted terrible corruption in high places—so long as the monster is fed. Yet with debt growing so much faster than money supply, the game can't continue.

What can the government do, though? At the slightest hint of inflation, (a) the bond market will crash, (b) the stock market will crash, and (c) interest rates will soar. Then (d) the housing market will crash, (e) people and companies won't be able to make ends meet, so (f) unemployment will skyrocket, and on and on. So expanding the money supply is like playing Russian Roulette with six live cartridges.

Yet if the money supply isn't inflated to catch up with debt, bankruptcies will multiply and rates will go up anyway. We're quickly coming to a point where there's no easy way out.

Feeding the Monster

Neither can we say that government is a disinterested party in this credit bubble. With huge debts of its own, the federal bureaucracy is in the same predicament that the average American household is in. It has huge debts to service, yet it wants to keep its spending binge going.

There seems little doubt that the credit bubble has to break. However, since the federal government has so much control over the economy, the real question is how the bubble can be broken while saving face and staying in business. To understand this, we must go back and look at the several cycles the government has gone through since World War II in trying to finance its operations.

The first cycle was one of relative fiscal responsibility. In other words, the government took in so many dollars in taxes and spent more or less the same amount.

One year might show a slight deficit, another might show a slight excess. In the end it balanced out, more or less. Federal debt remained fairly constant in this period, as is plain from Figure 3. Tax rates during this period were relatively high, ranging up over 90% in the upper tax brackets at times.

Fiscal responsibility broke down in the late 60's and early 70's, at least partially due to financing the Viet Nam war, and partly due to the increased demands of welfare payments under Lyndon Johnson's "Great Society." The political impact of raising taxes to cover these expenditures would have been too great, so alternate means of financing had to be developed.

At first the official price of gold was raised, and then the gold standard was abandoned altogether in 1971. That led to the second phase of financing, inflating the money supply. You can see the sharp up-turn of the Federal debt (Fig. 3) and the money supply (Fig. 1) in the mid- to late- seventies. This phase, however, led to wage-price inflation in the late seventies and early eight-

Fig. 3: Federal Debt, 1959-1997.

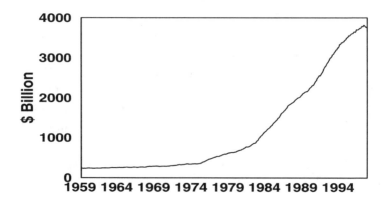

The Politics of Debt

ies. With government demands continuing to grow, and the specter of an inflationary economic collapse looming on the horizon, yet other means of financing the monster had to be developed.

The third phase of financing was the floating of government debt instruments, combined with the containment of price inflation. This is when the ratio of debt to money supply (Figure 2) began to climb. Although the money supply continued to expand, wage/price inflation was brought under control, and debt began to expand much faster.

Now, we are nearing the end of this third phase. Federal debt appears to be levelling off. The ratio of debt to money supply is declining. Major buyers of federal debt instruments are threatening to unload them and buy gold.[5] How will government continue to fund its ever-growing budget? Lacking the ability to exercize restraint and the political backing to raise taxes, phase one-style funding is no longer considered an option. Phase two-style funding would be suicide. To monetize the debt would send interest rates through the roof and collapse the economy and the dollar. What then? Something entirely new is needed—a fourth phase.

This fourth phase will inevitably be a return to financing government through taxes. When the free market won't pay the bill, government always turns to the captive market—the taxpayer. The problem is, raising taxes during difficult times without a war to justify it would be political suicide. That is where the cashless society would come in real handy. It would make possible a variety of "invisible" taxes whereby effective tax rates

---

5 The Japanese Prime Minister, in July, 1997.

could be hiked and taxes could be paid without taking obvious huge bites out of everyone's paychecks.

The Bug

Now, throw the millenium bug into this sticky problem. It will drive interest rates up for at least a short period of time—six months or a year. That alone could push our economy over the edge. Remember that a ¼% increase sent the Dow Jones Industrial Average spiraling downward in the spring of 1997.

Interest rate increases could be especially severe for an overextended government that is already approaching the threshold of debt that it can manage. And with over one third of the national debt financed at less than one year, rate increases will be *extremely painful*. How high might rates go on government bonds? Is some seemingly absurd figure like 30% really too high? Given the technical problems we face, given the specter of a banking collapse, a 30% rate for a one-year T-Bill may *not* be terribly unreasonable. It may be that the government will find that it cannot finance its debt even at that rate.

In short, the fiscal crisis we face due to the millenium bug won't just involve a banking crisis. It will be a fiscal crisis for the government. Again, it will occur in 1999, and not in the year 2000, and will accordingly be dealt with as a fiscal crisis, and not as a general computer crisis. The bug will bring the credit cycle to a premature end, and force government to finance itself with new kinds of taxes. These new taxes will require a whole new system for collecting them, as we shall see in the next two chapters. That's where the cashless society comes into play.

14. The Collapsing IRS

At present the United States has over $5.4 trillion in outstanding debt, mostly in the form of Treasury bills and bonds. All of this debt—about $20,000 for every man, woman and child in the country—has value because of the government's ability to force the people to pay taxes. This is the "full faith and credit of the United States government."

If the government found itself in a situation where it could no longer collect taxes, for whatever reason, it would be de-funded overnight. The only way it could pay its debt would be to create fiat money, either by printing it or electronically. To do that would be suicide, because government bonds would become almost worthless overnight, and nobody would buy any more. Funds would dry up instantaneously. Social Security, Medicare, food stamps and government benefits would evaporate like dew on a hot summer morning. Government employees would go home. And—probably—revolution would fill the air.

Such a situation would be terrible for just about everyone in the country. However, this is exactly what may result from the millenium bug—quite possibly before the change of the millenium. The reason is simple: right now, the IRS is the Achilles' heel of the entire United States government.

The Collapsing IRS

Off and on for the past 30 years, the IRS has been attempting to modernize their computer systems without success. The last phase of this modernization effort cost some $4 billion over a period of 11 years. This modernization has been a complete failure. In testimony before Congress, Arthur Gross, Chief Information Officer at the IRS, simply said IRS computers don't work.[1]

That's hardly any wonder. The IRS has an incredibly complex system of computers that is the result of successive attempts to upgrade and patch over many years, many administrations, and many tax code changes. They have over 63 mainframe computers in different locations, many horridly antiquated and out of date. For many of the programs they use, the software manuals and source code has been lost. The organizational chart for these computer systems is mind-boggling.

Now add the millenium bug to this mess. Not only are the IRS computers a tangled web of complexity, most of them are not year 2000 compliant. Far from taking the lead in making their computers compliant, the IRS has been fumbling around. They have not—as of the fall of 1997—even finished the assessment of their computers to figure out what it will take to make them compliant. This assessment phase involves typically about 1% of a total year 2000 project: awareness, assessment, planning, repairing and testing. However, Arthur Gross has publicly stated in the *Los Angeles Times* that failure to

---

[1] Shelly Davis, IRS Historian, Interview with Gary North, 1997. (Arthur Gross quit his job in exasperation in January, 1998.)

The Collapsing IRS

complete the year 2000 conversion "would mean a major disabling of the IRS."

Can it be done? Not likely. The IRS has 62 million lines of code that they know needs fixing. Their computers are already a disaster. Compare this to the Social Security Administration: They have only 30 million lines of code. They started on their year 2000 problem in 1989, and by mid-1996, they had 6 million lines fixed. Will the IRS do a bigger job in much less time? Given the raw numbers, serious doubts seem fully justified.

Add on top of this the fact that the IRS is hated, not only by the American people, but by Congress as well. The last time Congress seriously challenged the IRS and restructured it was in 1952, when political appointees were removed from low-level positions. Modern attempts to bring the IRS under Congressional scrutiny have been met with tax audits. At least one Congressman has landed in jail as a result. So even Congress has come to fear and hate the IRS. Only recently has the political need for republicans to take on the role of reformers brought the IRS into the limelight.

This loathing by Congress is surfacing in the computer crisis that the IRS is facing. Congress may prove unwilling to bail the IRS out of its troubles. In June, 1997, the IRS told Congress that it would need an additional $258 million for fiscal year 1998 to complete millenium bug fixes. This is over and above the $84 million requested in the budget passed by Congress. According to *Federal Computer Week*,[2]

---

[2] Elana Varon, "IRS seeks $258M more for Year 2000 solution", *Federal Computer Week*, June 23, 1997.

Senator Robert Kerrey (D-Neb) . . . told the senate panel that his group will recommend that the IRS be funded at its "current budget" for the next three years.

Committee members questioned whether the IRS should have any new funds, including the extra Year 2000 funds, before the agency outlines the return it expects to get from its investments. Sen. Richard Shelby (R-Ala.) lectured Summers and IRS officials for not complying with the Clinger-Cohen Act, which demands agencies show how their information technology spending will benefit their operations. "That's troubling, not just to me, but it will be really troubling to the American people," Shelby said.

James White, associate director for tax policy and administration issues with the General Accounting Office, testified at the hearing that Congress should consider not giving the IRS any of the money it has requested . . .

Has the IRS scaled back its requirements in the face of this negative response? Hardly. In September, 1997 they said they'll now need *$600 million* more than requested.[3]

It would appear the IRS is getting desperate. They are seriously facing the possibility that Congress will not fund their year 2000 conversion or further computer modernization programs. So in May, 1997, Arthur Gross issued a document called a *Request for Comments*. In it, Gross admits the extent of the agency's problems in all of their gory detail, then he states that the IRS is going to "shift responsibility for systems development and

---

[3] Sharon Machlis, "IRS Y2K woes cost more", *Computerworld*, September 15, 1997.

The Collapsing IRS 137

integration services to the private sector."[4] In other words, the IRS is admitting defeat and looking to outsource all of its computer systems, software design and maintenance to private industry. The purpose of the document is to solicit proposals from some well-heeled business that wants the job.

This is not a laid-in-concrete bid proposal yet. The IRS doesn't even know what kind of offers it might get. At this point, it's open to proposals. One thing it is asking for, though: the company that takes on this project must be willing to assume the risk of straightening things out. To quote Gross,

> "In general, the IRS seeks to create a business plan which shares risk with the private sector [and] incents the private sector to either share or assume the 'front end' capital investment."[5]

What is he saying here? Well, we know Congress is reticent to keep funding the IRS's techno-boondogles, so new funding isn't available. However, the IRS has a $1 billion/year budget for its information systems department. If outsourced, that money could reasonably be diverted to the winning bidder, but that winning bidder must fund the modernization with its own resources.

The IRS is seeking to award a contract by October 1, 1998, which includes implementing year 2000 compliance by June of 1999. Several large companies, including IBM, GTE, Hughes, Lockheed and Northrup, have expressed interest.

---

4 Arthur A. Gross, *Request for Comments for Modernization, Prime Systems Integration Services Contractor*, IRS Publication, May 15, 1997, p. 54.
5 *Ibid.*, p. 60.

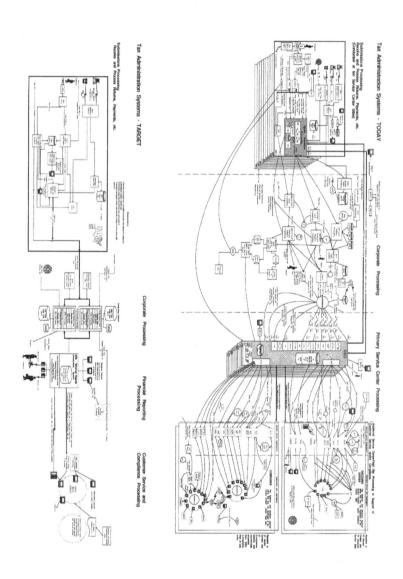

A Map of IRS Computer Systems

This document is nothing short of an all-out last-ditch-effort to resolve the problem the IRS is facing. With section headings like "The Next Eighteen Months: Staying in Business and Preparing for Modernization"[6] it appears to be just on the borderline of outright panic.

Why the IRS is the Achilles Heel

At present, it would appear that the IRS is in the worst shape of any government agency, both in its overall computer capabilities and its preparation for the year 2000. It is scrambling for some way to "stay in business."

Now, what happens when the American public gets hold of this? What happens when international investors find out what is happening? Will Americans, who hate the IRS more than any other government agency, who find its rules Byzantine in complexity, impossible to understand without expensive legal help, who find its methods of adjudicating disputes the epitome of totalitarian injustice—will such Americans see an opportunity for revenge? Will they stop paying their taxes the minute they think the IRS might not find out?

Realize that there are already millions of people who have opted out of the income tax system in the United States. Some of them do it as a matter of principle, citing detailed laws on the books, the Constitution, etc. Others—many of them educated into the relativistic values of the public schools—have simply decided that paying taxes is not one of their "values" and signed off. What

---

6 *Ibid.*, p. 14.

will it take to double that number, or worse? What happens when money is tight and revenues are down because of other economic shocks related to the millenium bug? How many more will volunteer out of our "voluntary" tax system?

Then what happens if investors figure all of this out? Will they want to be invested heavily in US debt when it all comes out in the wash? After all, if the IRS can't reasonably collect taxes, how is the United States going to pay its debts? Without a tax base, wholesale inflation is the only alternative. As a result, interest rates could skyrocket. What would be appropriate? 15%... 30%... More? It's hard to say. And as far as floating new debt, the government would be up the proverbial creek.

Realistically, there are two possible scenarios. One is that the IRS computers will break and revenues will dry up come April 15, 2000. Then the government bond market will collapse. The other is that investors will get wind of what's going on and sell off their US securities in order to avoid the risk, driving interest rates through the roof a year earlier. This might happen sometime in 1999.

Either way, if the government can't float its debt, it is dead. The whole bureaucracy will implode on itself within days, and quite likely the country will go up in smoke, as angry mobs are no longer pacified by their government payoffs.

Truly, the IRS is the Achilles' heel of the entire federal bureaucracy, and it's about to get shot.

What Does it Mean?

Many Congressmen could be aware of the situation and fully willing to let this situation play itself out. Ultimately anyone, be they an individual or a government agency, is going to reap what he sows. The strong-arm, merciless tactics of the IRS are going to put them in a position where they will receive no mercy when they most need it.

Talk of tax reform always seems to be short-circuited by the myriad of special interests who all want their piece of the pie. Just like the special interests that carve up the federal budget each year, these special interests jockey for tax write-offs, deductions, credits and favors whenever the subject of tax reform comes up. The result always seems to be tax laws that are more complex and sinister than before the "reform."

In a situation where the US government was actually facing a choice between real reform and collapse, real reform may actually take place. Given the IRS' multiplying computer problems, real reform could very well mean the end of that agency. Rather than being given the task of administering a new kind of tax, it would probably be allowed to die peacefully.

A number of alternative types of tax have been floating around in Congress already, including the flat tax and the value added tax which has become so popular in Europe. Whatever might take the place of the present income tax system, it would probably be much simpler to administer. That's the good news.

The bad news is that taxes will quite likely go much higher, and the new system will be designed to shield lawmakers from the political consequences of higher taxes. We discussed the need for a new method for funding the government in the last chapter. The voluntary capital of the bond market is going away. Taxes will have to take its place. The impending failure of the IRS makes the implementation of this new method of funding all the more urgent. It will be essential to the continued existence of the government. However, *the long-term need for the federal bureaucracy is to tax more, not less,* while studiously avoiding the political impact of raising taxes.

The income tax is well understood by the average taxpayer. As a result, raising income taxes has direct implications at the ballot box. Compare this with a value added tax. The average voter has no way to compare, say, a 15% value added tax with the income tax he pays now. He will find comparison difficult in the future if it is quietly built into the price of the goods he buys. As such, the political impact of such taxes is mitigated.

A cashless system offers the ultimate in taxation flexibility while minimizing political consequences. In a cashless system, taxes can be hidden in any number of places and paid automatically with the greatest of efficiency. Neither can they be easily escaped, since every financial transaction is a matter of public record.

In short, the urgent need to collect revenues while avoiding the political consequences thereof is a big reason that government should take an interest in a cashless society.

15. The Great Collapse of 1999

So is the millenium bug the gateway to the cashless society? Adding one thing to another, it may well be. It would appear that all of the ingredients for such a move are already in place:

- The millenium bug is a real problem that big companies and governments are very concerned about.

- The problems will not all be solved in time.

- Nobody really knows what damage it will cause. This permits all kinds of specualtion, ranging from the benign to the catastrophic.

- The possibility for mass panic as a result of a media-induced computer scare was demonstrated in 1992 during the Michelangelo scare.

- The banking system is highly leveraged and vulnerable to a scare.

- The government has already demonstrated that it will use a banking crisis to make major changes in the monetary system, and that it will seduce people into accepting those changes.

- The government is not averse to crises or even manufacturing the perception of a crisis. Rather, crisis is often an effective means to further the agenda of those in power.

- Powerful national, international and commercial interests are keenly interested in implementing an electronic money system.

- Key steps toward implementing the cashless society are already in place, or will be before the millenium bug hits.

- Government's ability to collect taxes and fund itself through the issue of debt instruments is failing. A new method of funding is desperately needed. The cashless society will make such methods possible in the long term.

In view of these many facts, it is hard to see a way to avoid a banking collapse and national emergency. In that emergency, the president will simply close the door to being able to withdraw cash from bank accounts, and like the emergency of 1933, his orders simply will not be rescinded after the immediate emergency is over.

Here is an imaginary scenario to describe how all of what we have been discussing might come together for the average man . . . .

Sunday, July 4, 1999

You've been hearing more and more news reports of bank runs in Europe and Japan for about a week. You've seen films of old ladies standing out in front of their banks crying, wondering how they're going to buy groceries next week. At 7:30 PM the President comes on national television to assure the American people that it can't happen here. He explains how the banking system

The Great Collapse

was designed to keep this from happening back in 1933, and lauds the excellent job that the Federal Reserve and the FDIC are doing. He outlines the government's plans and progress on dealing with the year 2000 problem which is causing concern about the banking system, and assures everyone that the banks will not be allowed to fail. You know the purpose of his speech is not merely academic. There's a lot of tension in the air, and he has a job to do. He must allay people's fears. You watch the talk with a somewhat cynical attitude.

Tuesday, July 7, 1999

At work, you hear someone saying they saw people lined up at the bank down the street when coming back a little late from lunch (and a trip to his own bank). You start looking around the office. People are quietly slipping out the back door and leaving. You go to your boss to ask for leave for a couple hours. His door is closed, the light is off. You, too, slip out and head for the bank, but you've got to stop at home first, since you didn't bring your passbook. At home, your wife is clueless that anything is going on. There was nothing on the noon news about any problem.

You make it to the bank, but the line is out the door. You quickly learn that they're not allowing withdrawals from savings accounts. You can only fill out a request for withdrawal, and you will be notified of the availability of the funds in 7 to 30 days. Withdrawals from checking accounts are being limited to $200 per person per day. You stay in line to withdraw your $200. Before you get to the window, the doors of the bank are locked. It's 4 PM—closing time. Everyone outside is told to go home. You were inside when the doors were closed, so you stay in line and collect your $200. It took three hours to get it, though. As you walk out, you see people sitting on the sidewalk outside the bank. Are they seriously going to camp out?

There's no mention of a problem on the evening news.

Wednesday, July 8, 1999

You call in sick to work, and go back to the bank first thing in the morning to get another $200. You're going to need it if the banks close. When you get to the bank, the line is four blocks long. You get in line.

Four hours later, you're still a block away from the door. Everybody in line is grumbling that they only have one teller at the window, a new one who is really slow. Then the announcement runs like a wave down the line: the bank is closing for lunch and will not re-open today. You hear a crash, then a cheer. Someone has thrown a rock through the front window. Some people start walking away. Others move up and sit down to wait until tommorrow.

Thursday, July 9, 1999

At 8 AM the President appears on national television to declare a national emergency and a banking holiday. All banks will be closed through the weekend, until the problem can be resolved. He asks everyone to remain calm and not to worry. The news is all over the television and the newspapers now.

The grocery stores that are still open are mobbed and sold out within an hour. Most businesses shut down and send their employees home. Isolated looting and riots break out in major cities, but quickly quelled by the police and the military.

Friday, July 10, 1999

Everyone stays home from work again. Only critical emergency services and utilities are kept running. All businesses are closed. Neighbors and churches share food with those who were caught short. All eyes are on the emergency session of Congress and the President.

Monday, July 13, 1999

At 8 AM the President appears on national television to announce an interim solution. While Congress is working on a plan, the Federal Reserve has reduced required reserves to zero. Solvent banks will be allowed to re-open to process checks and electronic transactions, however withdrawals of cash will be forbidden at least until the end of the week. Exchange controls are implemented whereby no money can be transferred out of the country without prior approval from the Executive Committe on the Financial Crisis.

The President salutes his decision as a brilliant interim solution to the problem, explaining how it will avert the economic devastation that even a one-week shutdown would cause.

By noon, most businesses have re-opened again. Retailers accept checks and credit cards, and typically offer a 10% discount for cash. Given such arrangements, most people find they can function. Hardest hit are the poor, who don't have bank accounts.

Friday, July 17, 1999

Another 8 AM television appearance by the President outlines the new plan adopted by Congress. He introduces the plan by condemning those who have caused the monetary crisis, saying it has been the result of unpatriotic mistrust. He explains how our economy is the foremost in the world, and it has been brought to its knees by a small group of selfish people who know nothing of how much progress has been made to resolve our year 2000 problems, and who do not care. Then he thanks the American people for pulling together so well in the past week, and says we will have to pull together some more to get through the problems we face.

Next, the President explains the difficulties associated with printing more cash to keep up with demand, and declares that it is not the duty of the government to satisfy unpatriotic currency hoarders, who are merely seeking unjust gain. He says the temporary system has worked quite well, and that with a little fine tuning, it will be able to carry us into the new millenium.

Invoking the War Powers Act, the President tells America that all Federal Reserve Notes must be turned in by depositing them in a bank account, opening one if necessary. The deadline for turning them in will be August 17, 1999, after which time they will be demonetized. This, he says, will mitigate the reasons for the bank panic, and stop currency hoarding and speculation. Coinage will remail legal tender, and properly licensed merchants will be able to obtain it from banks as usual.

Next, the President explains that in order to make the new system as widely accessible as possible, banks and the Visa/Mastercard network will be federally subsidized to provide accounts and Visa and Mastercard debit cards to low income households, and that businesses installing new credit card authorization terminals before the end of the year will receive a $2000 tax credit per terminal.

Finally, the President announces the formation of a new federal agency, the Monetary Policy Administration, to implement Congress' policies, and to make sure

The Great Collapse

the banking system will be year 2000 compliant before the end of the year.

July 31, 1999

During the past two weeks, the MPA has been established and begun examining year 2000 readiness. They announce that 30,000 programmers will be needed for a period of six months to make the banking system year 2000 ready. All programmers currently working in the banking system will now be under the authority of the MPA, so as to avoid duplication of efforts. 7000 more programmers will be recruited. Applications will be accepted immediately, with starting salaries at $750/hour guaranteed through January 31, 2000. (The salaries will be paid by expanding the money supply.)

September 15, 1999

Currency has been recalled, and the MPA is making good progress cleaning up year 2000 difficulties. The one problem area is check processing. Accordingly, the MPA has issued a briefing that banks will be held responsible for their own check processing software tools, and heavily fined for any delays or problems as a result of year 2000 bugs. The same day, many banks announce that check writing facilities will be discontinued. Other banks announce hefty charges to process personal checks.

December 15, 1999

The banking system is pronounced to be in good shape for the year 2000. Other sectors of industry, such as utilities and transportation, are receiving much more attention now, as they are not nearly so well prepared.

All eyes are off the banking system now, as people have quickly adapted to life without cash. Concern, however, is very high in other areas. What will happen in the next few weeks?

January 3, 2000

Problems due to the technical year 2000 glitch are assessed by the press as "moderate" and likened to a nuclear strike by a small nation. The Dow Jones drops 1500 points to the 2000 mark, as companies that did not adequately prepare realize how much trouble they are in. Electricity is out in about 10% of the country, and people are being told things should be back to normal in one to two weeks. Some telephone services are still in operation, however call volume has been huge, and people are being advised not to use the telephone unless absolutely necessary. The monetary system seems to have largely survived so far.

16. Electronic Money and Slavery

Two factors will drive any nation that adopts an electronic money system toward greater and greater control, until it becomes, in essence, a slave-state. One of these is the will to power, the second is crime.

The Will to Power

The electronic money system is the natural culmination of trends that have been developing for over a century. These trends are toward greater control and regulation of our daily lives by the state.

In many ways, western society is already subject to controls that make our nations look more like modern slave-states than free countries. For example, most financial transactions are already licensed in a variety of ways. Most businesses have at least one license commonly known as a sales tax license, but officially titled a "transaction privilege license" or something like that—in other words a license to make financial transactions buying and selling goods. Likewise, licenses are required to hire employees, and so on. The employee needs a license called a Social Security Number in order to work, and so on and so forth. So just about every financial transaction you make today is already licensed.

Licensed privileges must not be confused with genuine freedom. Anything that is licensed, be it your ability to work or to conduct business, your ability to build a house or drive a car, or your ability to marry, is *not* freedom. A license means you need permission from the state to engage in that activity. The fact that such "privileges" are readily granted for small fees should not deceive us. Just try to operate without a license and see how the system fights you. The act of obtaining a license is an act of fealty, the act which a serf performed for his lord.

Likewise, we must understand that the state has abandoned individual property rights in favor of state sovereignty. The state claims absolute ownership of all property through eminent domain, through its ability to seize property, and through its ability to tax property (real estate taxes, estate taxes) and cause it to be forfeited if the tax is not paid. In effect, real estate is owned by the state, and leased to tenants for rent (property taxes).

These trends, which amount to the state claiming to be God, have been directing public policy for at least a century. (Official denial of a supernatural God's very existence by the state opens up the vacuum for a natural god—a vacuum that the state then attempts to fill.) The state that seeks godhood inevitably tries to copy His dominion. Not only does it claim the ultimate ownership of everything—just like God—not only does it attempt to provide for its citizens—just like God—it also seeks to establish a universal system which defines everything else, and from which escape is no more possible than escape from God's creation. This universal system, the state's universe, if you will, is an essential element in the quest for godhood.

The cashless society is likewise an essential element in establishing the state's universe. Once an electronic

Electronic Money and Slavery

money system is introduced, there will be no keeping anything private. Every financial transaction can be recorded, and will likely be tracked and analyzed by the government. Thus, the state will attain a degree of omniscience, just like God. To go further, once the monetary system becomes electronic, the whole concept of money as a universal medium of exchange can be done away with. Every transaction can be licensed so that no one can buy anything without permission. As such, the state will gain a new degree of omnipotence. Just like a vengeful God could lay you low through disease or kill you at a word, so the state will be able to shut you down, partially, temporarily, or permanently. A bureaucrat who doesn't like something you're doing will be able to demand that you report to a detention center, and you won't even be able to buy food until you get there and check in. Likewise, there is no escape from the system, without the state's permission. You needn't be allowed to transform your wealth into untraceable forms, such as gold. In this way, you can be forced to stay within the system and your children after you. In short, electronic money makes the entire economy into the state's little universe—a universe from which there is no escape.

Though some of this may seem far-fetched, remember that it is just the logical conclusion of a trend that has been around for a long time. Even the detailed licensing of individual transactions already has a precedent in American history. During World War II, all kinds of goods were rationed. During the war years, money *wasn't* a universal medium of exchange. For many everyday items, ranging from gasoline to butter, you also needed a license in the form of a ration coupon to buy what you needed. Again, bureaucrats arbitrarily ordered loyal American citizens—Japanese Americans—to report to detention centers during World War II. Any intelligent person should understand that actions of the past often form precedents for future action.

This kind of control could actually be implemented to avoid crisis in the countdown to the year 2000. For example, if people think the financial system is going to collapse, they will be only too eager to spend their currency (or their electronic-dollars) for tangible goods before it becomes worthless. Rationing basic goods and services could be introduced to stem such hoarding. Likewise, other crises that occur concurrently with the millenium bug could provide the excuse to institute rationing. For example, as I write, food reserves in the United States are lower today than they ever have been in the history of the country. By late 1999, if reserves continue to decline, food shortages could be reason for rationing.

An electronic money system not only permits government to exert total control in "crisis" situations. It also permits government to milk the people day-in and day-out, and silence any dissent with a strong hand. The US government is pursuing a fiscal policy that is—in the long haul—totally irresponsible. Essentially, it is guaranteeing its ballooning debts with its continuing ability to tax the people. Down through history, high taxes have been the number one cause of rebellion and the overthrow of governments. When taxes have exceeded bearable levels, the people have sought relief in any form they could find. Typically, the tax level at which people will rebel is on the order of 30%. The upper classes in most western countries are far beyond that rate already, but the lower classes are not. However, that is going to have to change in order to keep the government alive. The wealthy are already paying the great bulk of taxes. At present, the top 1% of all US taxpayers are paying 28.7% of all the taxes.[1] They cannot be squeezed much more

Electronic Money and Slavery

without fundamental changes. Already, many of them are leaving the country to escape taxes. The great, relatively untapped pool of lower income taxpayers must be milked in order to meet the budgets of the future, while the most productive elements of society must be taken captive before they can be taxed more.

The federal government is fully aware of this fact. In the 1994 budget for the United States, it was stated that the average total lifetime tax rate for a child born in that year would be 82% of his income. This is what the government will need from him in income taxes, estate taxes, sales taxes, and so on, to continue in existence. And that is not only probably conservative, it just the average. Some will undoubtedly be taxed closer to 100%. Some will be taxed less.

Yet, to impose an average tax of 30% generally leads to revolution. That is an historical fact. Government planners are not ignorant of it. So, to impose huge, confiscatory taxes they need (a) a method to control people so they will not rebel, and (b) a method to hide the fact of the tax. An electronic money system provides just the answer.

The electronic money system is the ideal medium for both controlling people and hiding taxes.

An ideal electronic money system makes the economy into a little universe from which escape is difficult or impossible without government permission. To make escape impossible for the average person, the government must shut down the domestic black market, and at the same time regulate emigration by licensing all trans-

---

1 James Dale Davidson, William Rees-Mogg, *The Sovereign Individual* (Simon and Schuster, NY:1997) p. 117.

fers of money out of the country. Then the only way to escape is to run away and make an entirely new start from scratch. Right now, there are few places in the world where the average person, deprived of every last cent, would be welcome. Likewise, anyone who dared to publicly voice dissent against the system could be shut off and forced to report to the nearest detention/reeducation center immediately.

An electronic money system also gives government a total, instantaneous control over the money supply. Given that, it can fund itself by adjusting that money supply in a variety of ways. The crudest way of doing so is simply by printing money to pay bills. Electronic money provides the ultimate in such capabilities. Taxes are then merely a means of social control. They allow the government to fine-tune the economy. Savings rates versus consumption rates can be influenced with sales and income taxes. The relative wealth of various segments of the population can be adjusted through wealth redistribution, and so on. With an electronic money system, taxes can be hidden in almost any transaction you choose without your knowledge or consent. They can be built into the entire system and work silently, just like the laws of physics work in the universe.

Again, *what we are talking about here is just the logical conclusion of trends that have been growing for a long time.* With the advent of fiat currency in the past century has come the statist idea of exchange controls. Through such controls, citizens of various countries have been held captive by their governments, unable to invest money overseas, to buy overseas goods, or to escape from their country. That's possible because their money—which is inherently worthless—cannot simply be exchanged for other currencies. Again, hiding taxes in a variety of ways has become routine for taxing authorities. For example, employers are normally required to pay hidden taxes on an employee's wages over and above what they withhold from paychecks. The employee doesn't see these taxes on his withholding statement, but they directly reduce what he is paid for his services.

The establishment is well aware of how to fund government with hidden taxes using the money supply. It has been explained by past Federal Reserve Chairmen,[2] and the mechanics of it is straightforward. As we have already discussed, some radically new method of financing the government is going to be needed very soon. We are at the end of the credit cycle, and tax collection mechanisms are breaking down at the same time. Building (higher) taxes into the monetary system so that they aren't even seen may be the very thing needed.

In looking at the mini-universe that the state will create with an electronic money system, one has to wonder whether it does not pave the way to the ultimate slave-state.

We tend to think of someplace like the Soviet Union under communism as a slave state, so it behooves us to consider whether we would be any better off. That is really questionable. Already we are faced with illusions of freedom and ownership that have replaced the real thing in our country and around the world. We have titles to property we don't really own and never can own. We own businesses and take jobs that are controlled and

---

[2] Beardsley Ruml, "Taxes for Revenue are Obsolete", *American Affairs*, January, 1946.

licensed. We build wealth with money that has no intrinsic value.

What happens when we add on top of this a money system that allows total control of each individual, and which binds him and his children after him permanently to that system? What happens when we add an 82% tax rate built right in to the economy, just like it was in the USSR? The illusions will no doubt remain, as they are essential to the performance of the system. People who know they are slaves generally don't perform as well as those who think their labors will be rewarded. Yet the essence of slavery is that one is bound to do his master's will, and he has no power to make himself free without his master's consent. Whether that master gives his slave an easy time or a hard time doesn't make that slave more or less of a slave. He is still a slave, bound to his master's will. So, once the mechanisms of total control are in place, it doesn't matter whether the state exercises them with rigor all the time. The fact that the mechanisms are in place and there is no way out means that the one subject to them is a slave. That slave can be given a long leash and allowed to enjoy himself, or he can be forced to wear the mark of the beast and sent to the salt mines—at will. This is the real perversity of an electronic fiat money system.

Crime

Let there be no question: intangible money is always easier to steal than hard money. Granted, a crazed junkie with a gun won't come through your bedroom window in the night to rob your e-money account. However one must always be aware that education does not beget morality. Scoundrels are becoming more and more sophisticated in a sophisticated world, and for those with

Electronic Money and Slavery

the technical know how, stealing money could never be easier. Even with the electronic transfer systems we have today, millions can disappear in the blink of an eye. Citibank found that out the hard way a couple of years ago, when Russian hackers gained access to the bank and transferred more than $10 million to themselves by remote control. It is rumored that a number of banks have had huge losses as a result of electronic breakins, but they don't even dare to report them to the FBI, lest confidence in their institutions should falter.

Already, electronic money-related crimes have hit consumers hard. Credit card fraud is a $2 billion/year problem. Credit cards are the best pickings a pickpocket could hope for if he knows how to use them fraudulently. It's not uncommon to find somebody carrying around credit cards with $20,000 or more in purchasing power in their pockets.

An all-electronic money system will open up whole new realms for abuse. The only way to stem that abuse is through control. As such, market forces will drive controls on the electronic money system just as surely as they are driving the move to electronic money in the first place. People will want controls to make sure their money isn't stolen, pure and simple. For example, an anonymous cash card isn't exactly ideal. The thief that steals your wallet or purse might think so if he finds a cash card with a couple hundred dollars in value on it, but you will at the same time wish there was some way to turn the card itself off, and keep your money.

How much worse would it be if somebody could get hold of your bank card and take every last penny you own in a matter of minutes because all of your money is electronic? This consideration alone means powerful identification systems are going to be needed to protect electronic money. There is just no way around it. The market will demand it.

Identification systems are increasingly going high-tech. The systems of the future will undoubtedly include biometric information, such as fingerprints, retinal scans and more, probably stored on the microcomputer in a smart card.

Computer hackers can even crack smart cards, though. In September, 1997 some hackers announced they had cracked the leading smart card on the market today, the so-called Mondex card. It was done by examining the chip with an electron microscope. Technology tends to drive a vicious cycle between the thieves and the guardians of society, where the thieves crack the current technology and the guardians dream up ever more complex schemes to keep the thieves out.

What is the end of all of this? Probably an electronic device, that is implanted in your body that will provide real-time biometric identification, along with information about your emotional state. Such a device could both positively identify you, and recognize whether you are under duress, either because someone is forcing you to make a transaction you don't want to make, or because you are doing something illegal.

So the slave state will be able to monitor not only your money, but your very feelings when you make a transaction.

17. Resistance

Resistance to the implementation of an electronic money system will come from three quarters:

1) Those with technical misgivings—will the bug be fixed in time?

2) Those who love freedom and consider electronic money to be a gross invasion of privacy.

3) Those who object on religious ground and see it as a step toward the demonic economy of Revelation 13:16-18.

It is important to understand how this resistance is likely to be met, especially for those who might choose to resist. The methodology will probably be that of the carrot and the stick—just as it was in 1933. In other words, there will be enticements to join the system, and punishments for refusing to do so.

In considering resistance, understand that almost every one is going to get hit hard in his or her pocketbook. As such, the real resisters are going to be few in numbers. Most people will grumble a bit, but they'll go along in order to be able to access their money. Most people in our country have already been reduced to the state of slaves, economically speaking. They live hand-to-mouth and simply can't afford to have their savings (or even a month's worth of income in their checking account) wiped out. They can't afford to have their mortgages called, etc. They will readily forfeit their freedoms just to keep their heads above water economically. This basic fact means that the vast majority of people may pay lip service to resistance, but in the end they'll go with whoever controls their purse strings. In any event, let's consider how the government and society will likely deal with the three basic groups of resisters.

Those with Technical Objections

The people who are most concerned about whether the millenium bug will be fixed in time will be the ones who have successfully pulled their money out of the bank, etc., in time. As such, they will be the least likely to have their eyes clouded by the love of money. However, these people will also be the ones who caused the bank run.

Even though taking your money out of the bank is a perfectly sensible thing to do in consideration of what is likely to happen, people who actually do so will be demonized. They will be called "currency hoarders," "gold bugs," etc. Such "crimes against society" can and have been made illegal by presidential executive order. Do not doubt that currency hoarding and precious metal ownership will be outlawed when the electronic money system comes. Such activities will certainly come under the War Powers Act of 1917, as modified in 1933. Most likely, such "crimes" will also be considered "money laundering"—a vague crime with draconian punishments already on the books. And since bank records are public records, the regulators will know exactly who caused the bank run and who is likely to have a stash of

Resistance

currency or gold. Such people could be singled out for special attention. They may be asked to re-deposit their money or risk jail or forfeiture of all their assets, automatically and without trial. If the government is facing a credit crunch, they may simply face forfeiture without warning.

The majority of people who object to an electronic money system out of concern for the millenium bug will not have been concerned enough to get their money out of the banks before the bank run hits. They'll be very concerned when they see what happens, but their interest will primarily be to maintain access to their funds. In as much as the bug represents a threat to their funds, they'll be concerned about it.

Here we are talking about a large (i.e. politically significant) group of people who are primarily motivated by financial concerns. As such, the government will not demonize them, but pander to them. First, we will probably hear many, many official assurances that disruptions due to the millenium bug will be minor and temporary. These will come both from government sources and industry.

Second, efforts to make sure that the disruptions really are minor and temporary—especially disruptions in the new electronic money system—will be redoubled. America will be geared up for war—not a war against the "evil empire" or to whip inflation, or a war on drugs—but a war on the biggest computer bug of all time.

This war-like effort to resolve millenium problems will probably include invoking Executive Order 12919. Section 602 of this Executive Order allows "The head of each department or agency assigned functions under this order . . . to employ persons of outstanding experience and ability without compensation and to employ experts, consultants or organizations." In other words, every computer programmer in the country could be forced to leave his normal job and come work on the problem for the government. While the Executive Order allows employment without compensation, that probably won't happen. In all likelihood the programmers would be paid pretty well, e.g. above the going market rate even in the crisis. That way, they'd be happy with the arrangement and do a good job. If they were simply forced to work without pay, they'd make sure the job didn't get done—or put logic bombs in their code. This is one of the carrots that the government would offer programmers.

This way, news reports could be filled with eager programmers working busily to fix the problem. These would undoubtedly inspire public confidence. Remember that people will even believe a lie if told often enough. If reassured by federal officials often enough—even by federal officials who have no clue what will really happen—most people will believe it. If the situation is handled forcefully, perhaps by invoking the Executive Order, yet benevolently, paying programmers well for their help, the general reaction cannot help but turn from worry to sincere hope.

Lovers of Freedom

A whole different class of people who will object to the cashless society are those who are concerned that their freedoms are being eroded. The electronic money system will be seen by many of them as a gigantic leap toward control and slavery.

Now, if national governments weren't so eager to control people and monitor them, an electronic money system would be an opportunity to restore privacy in the

Resistance

financial system, rather than destroy it. At the same time, a country could actually boost its tax revenues and strengthen its economy. Private electronic money schemes have been detailed in the academic literature, and implemented on a limited scale.[1]

These electronic money schemes use cryptography, the science of codes, to create electronic currency that can function almost like paper currency. In some ways, it is even better than currency. Using it, a person could open a bank account anonymously, make anonymous withdrawals in e-currency, and spend that e-currency just like money. The merchant who receives the e-currency would not need to know the identity of the person who gave it to him in order to deposit it in his bank account, and even the merchant need not make his identity known to his customer. In short, these cryptographic electronic money schemes could insure complete privacy in every aspect of a transaction, customer-bank, customer-merchant, merchant-bank.

Even better, governments could license the creation of e-currency and collect a small fee from banks as they create it. Or governments could collect a small fee on each transaction with the e-currency. These small fees alone could add up to more than current tax revenues, even if they were on the order of a half-cent per dollar, or five cents per transaction.

But don't hold your breath. Most modern governments are too bent on controlling people to even consider such a possibility. Some small tax haven somewhere may

---

1 See Peter Wayner, *Digital Cash* (Academic Press:1997) for a technical discussion of the various electronic money systems possible.

have the unction to implement such a system, but don't expect any of the major first-world nations to do it. More likely, they'll make the use of such systems entirely illegal, and commercial entities (all government licensed) will eagerly comply.

It is conceivable that the government may make some limited and temporary concessions to privacy advocates. Typically, the National Security Agency is consulted in all matters concerning cryptography, and they may put together a fairly secure electronic money system for the country. However, such a system would certainly include a method whereby government agents could find out all the details they ever wanted to know about one's financial transactions, though perhaps a court order would be required to gain the necessary cryptographic keys to do any snooping.

Note that the FBI, backed up by President Clinton, is already proposing that such a "cryptographic key escrow" system be implemented for all cryptographic messages transferred on the internet, etc. Its application to electronic money would be included. Privacy advocates have strongly opposed such systems because they give government snoops unlimited power from a technical standpoint. At the same time, privacy advocates have only limited support in Congress. For example, Congress has not been willing to remove current restrictions on cryptographic software which government agencies cannot crack. Bills introduced by congressmen sympathetic to freedom are routinely subverted in committee.[2]

---

[2] To keep up on the political side of cryptography, check out the Electronic Frontier Foundation (www.eff.org) and the Electronic Privacy Information Center (www.epic.org).

Resistance

Another scenario is more likely than concessions to privacy advocates, however. Patriots who love freedom enough to speak out against electronic money may be demonized and marginalized. Consider the fact that in the past ten years all kinds of terrible, freedom-destroying legislation has been passed in the United States without any serious public discussion of the fact that it is destroying our freedoms. In the wake of such silence, we have been given laws that allow the government to seize our property without trial or accusation, to tap our phones, to take away our right to freedom of speech, the right to peaceably assemble, and so on. Those who have been concerned about freedom have been branded as right-wing extremists and considered a danger to the country. Anyone who speaks against electronic money from the point of view of freedom is liable to get similar treatment.

This branding has two effects: First, it causes people to distance themselves emotionally and intellectually from anyone who gets so branded. That person becomes a right-wing fanatic, somebody to stay away from, rather than somebody who has important ideas that need to be considered. Second, branding people like this tends to silence the like-minded. People may agree with the vocal defenders of freedom, but they will be afraid to admit it, much less speak out themselves, or otherwise support those who do speak out.

Demonizing one's critics has become very popular in the United States, and the left, in particular, has become expert in its use. Chief examples of targets have been white "racists" (in the civil rights movement), white males (in the feminist movement), heterosexual "homophobes" (in the homosexual movement), and militias (in the gun control movement). This list could go on and on.[3] The technique is quite common, and when 98.8% of the people in the country just want to get at their money, it will be an ideal time to demonize those who erroneously think freedom still means something.

Religious Objectors

The final group which may provide some resistance to an electronic money system are so-called conservative Christians. Many Christians believe that we are living in the last days, just before Jesus returns to establish his kingdom on earth. This period is described, often in very mysterious language, in the book of Revelation. In Revelation 13:16-18 we read:

> "And he causeth all, both small and great, rich and poor, free and bond, to receive a mark in their right hand, or in their foreheads. And that no man might buy or sell, save he that had the mark or the name of the beast, or the number of his name. Here is wisdom. Let him that hath understanding count the number of the beast, for it is the number of a man, and his number is six hundred threescore and six."

This is the demonic economy of the last days, which concerns many Christians. Presently, many understand that this prophecy will be fulfilled in an electronic money system coupled with some kind of ID system that might take the form of an implanted microchip. The book of Revelation goes on to warn believers against accepting this system in the strongest possible language:

> "If any man worship the beast and his image, and receive the mark in his forehead or in his hand, the same

---

3 An excellent book on the subject is Lawrence Dawson's *The Death of Reality* (Paradigm Co., Boise, Idaho:1996).

shall drink of the wine of the wrath of God, which is poured out without mixture into the cup of his indignation; and he shall be tormented with fire and brimstone ..."4

On this basis, a refusal to submit to the demonic economy is absolutely essential for believers.

Whatever you may think of Christianity or these passages of the Bible, understand that at least 70% of the population of the United States considers itself Christian, and of that number, a great majority certainly do believe that these scriptures could be fulfilled at this time. Such large numbers could be a force to reckon with in the event of a banking collapse and subsequent attempt to institute an electronic money system.

On the other hand, many modern Christians are fair-weather friends of Christ who have gotten used to being entertained in church, and who have never made a decision as a matter of faith that cost them dearly, much less faced real persecution. Whether they will rebel against the implementation of an electronic money system, especially when their pocketbook is involved, is highly questionable. Much of the answer to this question depends on how pastors and televangelists will respond.

Certainly there is considerable room for pastors and evangelists to back down from the idea that a cashless society is the beginning of the demonic economy. For example, in all likelihood, the electronic money system will be initiated with some kind of credit card or smart card. It will not involve tattooing or microchip implantation, at least not at first. As such, one could certainly argue that such a system isn't the same as taking the mark

---

4 Revelation 14:9,10

of the beast, and buying into it won't bring the wrath of God.

Again, many Christians already believe that the prophecy concerning the mark of the beast will not happen until after a "rapture" in which Christians are taken out of the earth. As such, they will reason that they don't have to be concerned about electronic money or anything that happens before the "rapture."

So there is certainly room to interpret or re-interpret scriptures to accommodate government-mandated changes in the economy. The economic pressure to do exactly this will be intense, especially for large churches and national ministries. Those who have regular television or radio bills will not be able to pay them unless they join the system. As such, the voices of those who oppose the changes will be cut out of the electronic media overnight. Only those who have compromised will be left. Again, large churches, which are dependent upon large incomes, and are often in debt for their buildings, will be forced into positions of compromise by economics. Those who will not compromise will watch their funds dry up instantaneously because 98.8% of the people will only have electronic funds to give. Big churches will "go out of business" overnight.

One also has to remember that the great majority of churches are incorporated as charitable entities and licensed in a variety of ways. The difficulties that such a church would face should it decide to opt out of the electronic money system would be innumerable. Everything from its tax status to its property and bank account would be up for grabs.

As such, it is really questionable whether the Christian community will present any kind of effective resistance to an electronic money system. With voices against the new system silenced by economic means, the compromising and acquiescent will rule the day. The real moral argument against the cashless society—that it condemns the innocent and crushes the weak will be lost in the shuffle.

If any effective resistance occurs, it will most likely come from two quarters: (1) the LDS church (Mormons), and (2) churches where pastors have adequately prepared their congregations, especially if the pastor is not completely dependent upon church income for sustenance. Since LDS members materially prepare for an end-times tribulation by storing food, etc., they will be in a good position to opt out of the cashless society, given, of course, that church leadership so directs. Their ministers are also bi-vocational.

On a national level, however, both of these groups are a small minority. Such believers, like their patriot cousins, can be demonized, marginalized, and lumped in with currency hoarders and gold bugs. This will not be hard to do in a society where anyone who actually lives differently based on their (Christian) faith is thought to be somewhat strange by conservatives, and an "intolerant right-wing Christian bigot" by liberals. None the less, moral convictions are the only basis upon which strong, sustained resistance can be mounted.

A Word to the Wise

When this monetary crisis occurs, you will be called upon to abandon or compromise your beliefs, be they religious, patriotic, or simply matters of common sense. In that day, what you believe is right and true will be called evil and unpatriotic. Many people will undoubtedly compromise, and change what they "believe" out of convenience' sake. They will submit to the coercion. They will bite on one of the carrots offered them by the government. They will, like Esau, sell their birthright[5] for a mess of porridge.

If you are really intent on resisting the changeover to an electronic money system, I would encourage you to consider carefully how you are going to respond *now*, before the crisis hits, and prepare for it. If you find yourself in the middle of it, unprepared, the temptation to compromise will be all but unbearable. You will have to resist the government. You will have to resist the temptation to do evil. The unjust steward will come to you and ask you to cut your debts in half so you will give him favor.[6] And as far as *public* opinion goes, you'll find yourself outnumbered 100 to 1 or even 1000 to 1. Here and now you can see clearly. When the cost for seeing clearly goes sky high because you haven't planned, don't assume you'll be able to.

So count the cost and get ready for it. Even if the millenium bug isn't the catalyst, you know such things are coming in the next 20 years, so your efforts in preparing will not be misspent.

There are two ways in which resisters might gain a victory: One is if the technical end of the millenium bug proves too much for the system to handle. If, come January 3, 2000, the monetary system is in ruins and nobody has any money at all, the result could be a complete overthrow of the governments that went this route. Of course, those governments are going to work hard to make sure that doesn't happen—their first prior-

---

5   You might ask, what is your *birthright*? Certainly we might say one aspect of it is sound money made out of gold and silver. That much is guaranteed in the Constitution as a birthright to every American.
6   Luke 16:1

Resistance

ity is their own survival, even if it means being transformed into a demon in the process. I've been intimately involved with terribly run companies that have sustained terrific damage from both without and within, and it's amazing how they can survive and survive when they really deserve to die. This applies all the more so to governments. So the hope of complete collapse seems remote, if not absurd.

The second way to gain victory is slowly. In the immediate aftermath of the switchover, real resisters would be best advised to lay low. Public opinion will turn against them strongly, for the reasons outlined above. However, with time the real issues behind an electronic money system will settle in, and people will wonder why they ever bought into it. As people see how it enables the state to monitor every aspect of their lives and control them, as they see how it enables the state to tax them at rates upwards of 80%, they will learn to hate it. The resisters who succeed at remaining outside the system will then find a growing sympathy to their arguments. If they can also help others get out of the system, their numbers could swell to the point that they might have the power to change things.

The Millenium Bug

18. The Black Market

Politically significant opposition to the cashless society in the midst of an economic crisis is probably nothing more than a vain dream. The people who might fight it will be demonized and silenced in a variety of ways. Such will be the case even though many people will absolutely hate the all-electronic money system for a variety of reasons.

However, because people will find the cashless society distasteful and intrusive, it is possible that a black market will thrive in a cashless society. This black market will be the only way to accumulate any wealth whatsoever that is not controlled, licensed, and ultimately owned by the state. So the black market will be synonymous with freedom and liberty, rather than criminality. If taxes are high, the motivation to do some off-the-books trading will be greater still.

This black market will be like other black market economies which develop from time to time, when government regulation outlaws the normal dynamics of free markets. A few people can live entirely within such black markets, while many others dabble in them occasionally.

For example, an underground auto mechanic or carpenter may be able to make a great living charging far less than the equivalent person in the system. He will not be subject to regulation and increasingly heavy taxation. He will not have to insure himself against lawsuits in a system where purchasing his services would be illegal to begin with. So to hire him, instead of paying his employer with e-dollars, you go to the grocery, buy a little more than you need, and pay him directly with food. You save 80% of the cost of repair on your car, and he puts twice as much in his pocket as would an ordinary above-ground mechanic.

Take certain religious groups, like the Amish, who shun modern conveniences as a model for how the black market might work. Such people might not own telephones themselves, but they are not afraid to use a pay phone, or a neighbor's phone, if they need to make a call. In the same way, people who primarily live in the black market may not use electronic money, but they may need a friend's help from time to time to make an electronic transaction. For example, one probably won't be able to pay property taxes any way but electronically. However, a black-marketeer could perform a service for someone and ask them to transfer some funds to the county assessor to the credit of his account as payment.

Any kind of government crackdown on the black market will probably take some years to develop, just as the black market itself will take some years to develop. Whether the government will crack down on the black market, and how hard, largely depends on public perception of that black market. If it is equated with freedom and independence, and a lot of people trade in it on the side, shutting it down could be political suicide. On the other hand, one of the long-term goals of those who seek an electronic money system will undoubtedly be to paint the black market in the blackest terms possible. If public opinion can be swayed against it, then the harshest imaginable measures can be brought to bear on it. Like drug dealers, black marketeers would be subject to total

The Black Market 177

confiscation of all that they own, and harsh prison sentences. Technologically speaking, the government could certainly apply some formidable tools to shut the black market down. With every bit of financial data for every single person available in electronic form, sophisticated analyses could be employed to determine if a person is trading in the black market or not. Let's go back to the black market auto mechanic as an example of this: Suppose you buy a car. The make and model of that car is public information. Statistically, we can say that this car will need such-and-such maintenance and repairs over a period of so many years. Monitoring your finances, the government can determine if those repairs were made. Was the timing belt changed at 70,000 miles? Did you pay someone to do that? Or did you buy the belt to do the job yourself (provided you have the skill to do it)? If not, then an analysis program can raise a red flag. More careful analyses can be performed. A case against you can be built by a computer a thousand miles from where you live, and that case might be enough to put you in jail all of a sudden, without a moment's warning and without trial.

Let there be no doubt that a determined government could quash a black market in a cashless economy, only provided that public opinion favored it. So the question becomes, how determined will the government really be, and where might pockets of resistance form?

If anything deters the government from a serious effort to route out the black market, it may be the "criminal" element. Street gangs and drug lords do a booming business, and they have already corrupted many politicians and law enforcement officials with bribes and threats. Their trade would not be possible in the above ground economy, so they would be part of the underground. While unsavory, alliances between such gangs and religious or freedom-oriented resisters would probably form. Public officials and law enforcement could be bought off just as they are now.

Likewise, localized pockets of resistance could develop in some communities. A strong church in a small community could conceivably influence local officials to turn their heads, especially if those local officials were members of the church. Without local eyes, ears and guns, a federal bureaucracy may be ill-equipped to rein in an underground economy. Such a scenario could especially develop in many small western communities which are dominated by the LDS church if encouraged by their leadership.

19. Personal Preparedness

This chapter is primarily addressed to those who find the cashless society distasteful, and who wish to draw the line and bow out, if and when it comes. To do that with a minimum amount of pain, you're going to have to get ready now. None the less, even if you don't care about whether we go cashless or not, read this chapter. You will be much better off if you have some foreknowledge of what might happen and how to respond to it. There will be some tremendous profit opportunities here for those who understand what is happening, and the person who doesn't care about the cashless society will be in the best position to take advantage of them, provided he is prepared.

Making Some Decisions

In planning for coming events, the first thing to do is to make some personal decisions. Are you willing to buy into the cashless society or not? If so, do you want to take advantage of the situation, and try to make some money? Or do you want to protect yourself against the technical aspects of year 2000 glitches? If so, you need to position yourself accordingly. If you can foresee later developments down the road of a cashless economy that are unacceptable (be it ID chip implants or an 80% tax rate), then will you have a back door—a way to bow out of the system later on? This too, may require some planning right now. Once you're a part of the cashless society, it may be hard to get out.

If you're not willing to be part of a cashless system, then you have to decide what action you'll take when it comes. Will you stay put, and hope to be a part of the underground economy? Will you go to another country where they don't have a cashless society?

If you make these decisions now, set some goals, and work toward them, then you'll be able to do what you want to do when the time comes. If you don't think about it and don't plan, then others will decide your future for you, pure and simple.

And it is always best to have more than one alternative available. If you think "the cashless society is okay," but you don;t find out until several years later that you're going to get astronomical taxes along with it, you might get stuck without a viable back door. If you decide to be a part of the underground economy, but you don't foresee the fact that the government will enact the death penalty for participating in it, you might get herded into the cashless society anyhow, or go down in flames resisting. If you decide you'll leave, and go to such and such a country, but the millenium bug turns that country into a hell hole, you might be faced with jumping from the frying pan into the fire.

There is also the possibility that the whole scenario I've outlined here will blow over and nothing will come of it. I don't think that will be the case, but I make no claim to be a prophet or a clairvoyant. What then? You don't want to bet your life or your life savings on the idea that these things must happen.

Personal Preparedness

You have to weigh these things and make some decisions based on your principles, your faith and your finances. If you do it now, and do it well, you'll have nothing to regret in the days to come, and you'll expand your horizons besides.

Getting Your Assets Ready

The first thing to do to prepare for a banking collapse is to reduce your exposure to the banking system. To do that, you'll have to divest yourself of electronic assets. In other words, anything that is merely a ledger entry in some computer. Bank accounts are the ultimate electronic asset. They represent "dollars" that aren't there and that have no intrinsic value even if they did exist. However, don't neglect things like retirement accounts, brokerage accounts, whole life insurance policies, and so forth. Things like stocks must be understood primarily as electronic assets too. Although a stock represents real tangible assets, with stocks trading at multiples of book value, and your ownership of it proven by a data record in some computer, it is essentially an electronic asset.

Think of it like this: if that asset can be held hostage by a banking collapse, it's an electrcnic asset. If you cash in your mutual fund, you're going to get a check in the mail. You have to take that to the bank. If the bank is closed or the bank has gone all-electronic, then your assets are stuck in the system.

You're going to have to decide how far to go in this. Weigh the risks and the potential rewards for yourself. Personally, I don't think it makes any sense to keep a lot of money in the bank for the next year or two at 0 to 5% interest. The risk just doesn't justify it. On the other hand, if you know you can double your money in commodities trading between now and July of 1999, it might be worth it to you to keep that account open. Again, many of us need the utility of a checking account, so it makes sense to keep one open with some funds in it, knowing we can pay the money out of it to cover bills even as the system is shutting down.

In evaluating your assets, remember that we are at the top of a credit cycle. (And with looming financial crisis in the far east, perhaps we are looking over the edge, even now.) As I write, stocks are at an all time high, and the banking system is more leveraged than it's ever been, debt is astronomical, but bonds are very high. In other words, paper or electronic assets are at their highest values, historically speaking. It may just make good economic sense to sell high and buy something else that's low, regardless of the millenium bug. If that something else is a tangible asset which is not subject to the vagaries of a computer bug, or the cashless society, all the better.

Now, for most middle class Americans, getting rid of their electronic assets will take anywhere from one to six months. Unless you have only a few dollars in the bank, you don't want to just close the account and demand a wad of cash. First of all, you don't want to be identified as one of those bad guys who started the bank runs. Secondly, you've habituated yourself to using a bank, and you aren't going to be able to change overnight. If you want to close other accounts, you'll need to keep the account to deposit checks in, etc.

Rather, what you should do is change your habits. Start drawing your account down, and depending on it less. Re-learn how to use cash instead of checks or credit cards. Reduce the flow of money through your account and you can maintain a lower balance. Change your habits slowly enough not to arouse suspicion, but at the same time, don't assume that the bank runs will wait for you to change.

Personal Preparedness

The first step you must take is to get into cash, i.e. paper money. If you have enough to think about investing in other areas, fine. We'll discuss that in a bit. However, the money you normally keep laying around in the bank or a money management fund or whatever for easy access should be turned to cash. If you do this much, you will have protected yourself from the bank runs. However, you won't have protected yourself from the cashless society yet. Remember, your cash is fiat money. It circulates as money as an act of faith in the government. The government can breach that faith at will.

Cash will be important for at least a short period surrounding the bank runs. However, anywhere from two weeks to two months after the declaration of a banking holiday, you may be requested to turn cash in or watch it become worthless. If you're opting out of the cashless society, you'll have to be out of cash before that happens. There will probably be a door open to redeem cash overseas after the domestic recall date, but getting it out of the country will be very difficult.

Investing for the Future

There are a wide variety of investments suitable for protecting oneself from potential year 2000 problems, be they technical problems or social ones. Basically, anything that is a tangible asset with intrinsic value is a possibility. Such investments don't depend on computers for their value, so they should survive a crisis.

Perhaps the most traditional of tangible investments are real estate and precious metals. Both of these deserve some detailed comment. However, there are plenty of other things one can invest in. In our age, we've learned to take a very narrow view of what an "investment" is. We tend to think of investments as things bought on stock exchanges or at the bank. You have to broaden your horizons a bit, and become more of an entrepreneur, in order to find tangible investments. For example, livestock can be a great investment. Or you might want to build up inventory in your business, or buy a business. If you anticipate power outages due to the technical aspect of the millenium bug, you might want to stock up on solar power equipment. Use your imagination. Do that on your own. Use your specialized knowledge and skills to find a niche where you can buy something that will probably go up in value.

Real Estate

Real estate bought in the right location has, historically, been a good investment. From the perspective of the millenium bug, urban real estate could become very risky. With the potential of utility outages, transportation gridlock, the failure of government payment systems, etc., cities could become centers of civil unrest. As people become aware of the potential problems, we could see falling prices on homes in 1999. And if civil unrest boils over, cities could become economically depressed for decades, as everyone who has the means leaves. Besides, the trend in population growth is already away from major cities.

Rural or small town real estate is a different matter. A relatively self-sufficient farm or ranch well away from the city could become a premium property in hard times, especially if it has some agricultural capacity.

The problem with real estate is that it can be held hostage to the government. That could be a concern if you're averse to the cashless society. To pay your property taxes, you will have to deal with someone who is part of the cashless system, but who isn't afraid to make

Personal Preparedness

a black market transaction. You provide him with some goods and services. In return, he transfers your property tax payment to the county. Then, when it comes time to sell your property, you'll have to sell it to someone who is not part of the cashless system if you want to remain outside the system. Finally, if the government cracks down hard on the underground, your property could be seized merely for participating in the underground economy. That should be a real concern in any country like the United States, where the government has no scruples about seizing property without even charging its owner with a crime.

So, in buying real estate, you have to keep in mind what your plans are to deal with the cashless society, and contingencies that might arise. Certainly, you don't want to keep all your eggs in one basket. Diversification is important in any investment strategy, and the millenium bug doesn't alter that fact. More comments on this in a moment.

Precious Metals

Precious metals are another traditional tangible investment, particularly gold and silver. In real terms, gold is trading at a 25 year low, and silver isn't too far behind, at this writing. With stocks at all time highs and gold at long time lows, common sense would suggest that one sell stocks high and buy gold low. A lot of big players are doing exactly that.

If you throw the millenium bug into this equation, precious metals look like one of the best deals around right now. And even those of very limited means can get into gold and silver. You can go buy silver if you've got $10 or $20 to spare, and gold if you have $200 or so.

With precious metals, there is the danger of confiscation if the cashless society is implemented. Frankly, I think that danger is limited, because the government will mainly be concerned with cash. Too few people own precious metals anymore for them to be the first priority as they were in 1933. None the less, you may want to consider the possibility of confiscation in advance. If you're planning to be part of the underground, you should make sure not to leave a paper trail on your purchases. (Ask your dealer what kinds of records he keeps, if any.) Then hide your gold carefully. Do not put it in a safe deposit box. If you have contingency plans to get out of the country, move your hard assets out before you go, so they'll be there waiting for you when you get there. You don't want to cross borders or travel in an emergency with anything more than money for the trip, unless you want it stolen by thieves or government agents who know lots of people are fleeing with everything they have.

Getting Ready for Life in the Underground

If you're planning to go underground, the sooner you find a like-minded group of people, the easier a time you'll have making the transition. When the crisis hits, if you are one isolated person who wants to go underground, you're going to have a hard time of it. You may even be forced to give up and give in to the cashless system. The key to surviving underground is to have a network of people you can barter with. Don't wait until you are in a pinch to find those people.

If you don't know people off-hand who are committed to an underground economy when a cashless society is implemented, then you're going to have to either find them where you live, recruit them where you live, or move. There are a number of possibilities for each of these options. Talk to various pastors in your area, and see if any of them are seriously preparing their people to face this issue. Or if there is a bartering group or cooperative in your area, that is a good place to start. If nobody is thinking along these lines, you might consider holding a seminar on the subject in order to find interested persons, and then informally organizing them. Finally, if you can't bring it together where you are, you might want to move. Don't just pack up and move without checking an area out. Obviously, you need to be able to secure your living where you are going, and wherever it is, you should be able to find those like-minded people there. You might check the newsgroup alt.barter on the internet.

I know of at least one Christian "covenant community" that is forming in Arkansas as an attempt to weather the storms that the millenium bug might cause. They are entrepreneurially oriented and working to build something that will prosper even in an all-out crisis where everything collapses, and yet do well if the whole problem blows over. This may be a viable alternative for some. (For more information, contact Bob Rutz, PO Box 25, Kingston, AR 72742, (800)972-7737.)

Once you have some people to barter with, you're going to have to learn to barter. Bartering isn't quite like walking into Walmart and plopping down your credit card. You should read the book Bartering Secrets. You also have to practice, so start now. Don't wait until you are forced to by circumstances.

If you are working a job, and your employer isn't headed underground along with you, consider the possibility of a cashless society to be an extra incentive to start a business on the side, and preferably one that is amenable to the underground. Realize that there is already a considerable underground economy in operation in the United States, especially for income tax reasons, and even books about how to get involved in it. (See the Resources.)

Leaving the Country

Keeping a door open to go somewhere that doesn't have an electronic money system may be wise, even if you don't have any intention of exercising that option right now. Maybe you'll never need to go. Having the option, however, could prove to be important insurance, and some planning is necessary if you want to be able to go. Some of this planning is ridiculously easy to do.

The first and simplest step is to get a passport so you can get out of the country if you need to. Right now, you have only to apply for it and pay the $60 fee. Don't put it off if you can foresee any situation in which you might want to get out of the country. Don't assume you'd be able to even take this simple first step in a crisis. Passport offices are not set up to handle the high volume traffic they might experience if there is a national emergency and lots of people want to leave.[1] In such a situation, you may find that you cannot even get a passport to get out of the country. Just the fact that the passport offices cannot handle the traffic makes this a certainty. Forget about the restrictions that might be imposed in a national emergency. This is basic A-B-C's, but most people who will want to leave in a hurry won't even be able to because they haven't taken the first step.

---

1   It used to be you could apply for a passport at any post office, but that was mysteriously stopped.

Personal Preparedness 189

The next step is to find someplace to escape to, if conditions so warrant. Pick a country where an electronic money system isn't likely, purely for technical reasons. First world countries are probably out. They're all going to be having the same problems, and they're all going to be trying the same solutions, perhaps in a coordinated fashion under control of the UN. Pick a second or third world country instead.

To pick a country may require a little research. There are two approaches you can take. One is to think of some places where you'd like to go and then research them. For example, if you know Spanish and you like South America then pick some countries and write their embassies and ask for details about immigration. Another approach is to find countries that are actively seeking immigrants of one type or another. For example, there are countries that take a great interest in American retirees, such as Mexico, Belize, and Honduras. These countries have American retiree communities and special provisions for permanent retiree visas, etc. Other countries are seeking people who can set up businesses and employ people. Again there may be someplace you can go where you have friends or relatives, and where it's relatively easy to get into the country, or a place you might wish to go as a missionary.

Remember that in a time of worldwide crisis, travel may be restricted. Countries that normally issue easy visas may not be so quick to do so in times of trouble. If you can afford it, do something to assure your entry into that country. You may be able to gain citizenship somewhere if you have ancestors from there. Alternatively, you may be able to buy a permanent resident visa or even citizenship in some country. These would pave the way for a smooth entry into that country even in times of trouble. However, they can be quite expensive. For example, a permanent residence visa in some central or South American country might require a permanent investment of $25,000 or more.

Unfortunately, most of us cannot meet the genetic or financial qualifications for immediate second citizenship somewhere. One alternative is to move now to a place that will grant citizenship based on residency. Get a job overseas. Go on a long-term mission trip. Likewise, buying property in that country will facilitate your entry during an emergency. If you are a respectable, tax paying land owner or businessman, you'll probably be welcome. In short, do what you can to make yourself a resource to that new country, and not a liability. Then you can say "see, I own property, I provide services, I pay taxes, etc.," and they'll see that they want you around.

You might be thinking that the idea of leaving the country is only appropriate for rich jet-setters. However, to most of the world, if you are an American and you are employed, you are a rich jet-setter. Property prices in most places are really quite reasonable compared to the US. Maybe not in downtown Paris or Tokyo, but you'll probably consider most ordinary properties in a second or third world country to be incredible bargains. For example, perusing real estate listings in Belize (a small english-speaking country in Central America), I find a 4 bedroom house with its own well on 30 acres, planted with citrus trees for $30,000. Or you can get 100 acres of unimproved but good quality land for $10,000. Then there is a farm for $60,000 whose produce will pay for itself in 2-1/2 years. Alternatively, you can buy a 2 bedroom beachfront house in Panama for $35,000. Or 10,000 acres of ranchland in Argentina for $10 per acre. The opportunities are out there. You just have to start looking around.

In the Midst of Crisis

You've heard about bank runs in Europe and Japan on the news for about a week, but things have been quiet at home so far. Politicians have been urging every one to keep calm. Then you learn it's started here. What will you do?

Hopefully, you've already minimized your exposure to the problem. This could be your opportunity for some windfall profits, if you play your cards right.

If you're not averse to the cashless society, you could hire a couple security guards and stand in front of the bank with a wad of cash and sell it to people for their electronic deposits (remember, the banks' computers will still be up and running at this time). The bank may well cooperate with you, especially if it's a small bank and you're acquainted with the manager. You accept the electronic deposits (e.g. checks, at a discount of anywhere from 2 to 1 to 10 to 1 and give people the cash they are so desperate for. For example, they write you a check for $200, you go to the window and deposit it, and hand them a $100 bill. That will more than make up for the interest you forfeited by keeping cash instead of bank deposits.

On the other hand, if you're averse to the cashless society, you might consider working with a local pawn shop instead, or working deals with businesses that seem to be in distress. People will be selling anything of value to raise cash, to anyone who has cash, and it will be the best of buyer's markets.

Anytime between a day and a week after the bank runs start, the President will declare a national emergency and a banking holiday. Our leaders will begin hammering out The Solution. Be aware that you'll need some cash paper money during this period to function.

Cash will be king then, not gold or silver, not barter: Federal Reserve Notes. People will be selling things to get cash. (Yes, gold and silver could even go down briefly during this period. You don't want to get caught having to sell then.) So you should keep enough cash to live for a month. That should bring you through the period when cash is king.

Sometime during this period is when a cashless society will be put forth as the answer, if it's going to be. A deadline may be established to turn cash in, after which it will be demonetized. You don't want to be caught with a lot of cash on hand if that happens. If you put it back in the system then, you'll have nosey bureaucrats after you since "hoarding" currency will be illegal. If you are opting out of the cashless society, you won't want to use worthless Federal Reserve Notes as fire starter, but that's about all they'll be good for.

Although demonetization of Federal Reserve Notes may not happen right away, if you see things headed toward the cashless society, understand that it would be unsafe to assume they won't be demonetized. As the deadline for demonetization draws near, they will lose value as people start to view them as problematic. You don't want to get caught holding the bag then. On the other hand, if we don't head toward the cashless society, you will want to hold on to your paper money until the millenium bug actually hits. If the money system really does go down, they will be the preferred medium of exchange for at least a while.

Truly, the period between when the bank runs start and the millenium bug hits will be interesting and dangerous. However, there will be some great opportunities for those who dare to seize the day. Remember Baron Rothchild's famous remark, the time to buy is when there's blood in the streets.

What if the Crisis Doesn't Happen?

Although I honestly think the crisis I've discussed in this book is all but certain to happen, we have to consider the possibility that it will not happen. What then? What if the banks get their computer problems fixed in plenty of time, and they avert a panic. What if the newspaper reports turn from alarm to glowing reports of success? What if it all blows over?

If you take some of the recommendations I've made here, and don't get crazy or stupid about it, but stay rational in your planning, you won't go too far wrong. If you sell electronic assets at all-time highs, and buy tangible assets near the bottom of their cycle, you've probably made a good investment decision by any standard of investment wisdom. It won't be a matter of life and death, or compromise with evil, that's all.

Likewise, if you buy some property overseas, and maybe do a little travelling, you will expand your horizons wonderfully. If the millenium bug doesn't drive you out of the country, but you have a nice vacation house on the beach that you can go to now and then, and that you can rent for a few hundred dollars a week to vacationers, that's not so bad. Or if you have a hundred acre farm that brings you $30,000 a year in income, who's going to complain about that?

Besides, if you've read this far, I trust you see how our nation is declining. You know the cashless society is coming, whether the millenium bug triggers it or something else does. You know we're losing our rights and our freedoms, as well as our morality. You see economic prosperity on the wan as both people and their government mortgage their future for present pleasures. So in times like these, it would be comforting to know that you aren't stuck where you are. When you're asked to do something disagreeable, or to keep your mouth shut when you know you shouldn't, or when your children are drafted to serve in some miserable foreign war, you won't have to just put up with it no matter what.

20. A Silver Lining?

In the next two years, the media is going to focus a lot of attention on the *technical* aspect of the millenium bug and the problems it will cause. It will not, however, focus a lot of attention on what its own coverage will do. Likewise, Congress and business will spend time focusing on the technical problem. As such, the *social* problem—the panic that could result—will go largely unaddressed until we are right in the middle of it. In such a situation, someone can step forward with "the answer" and it will be swallowed hook, line and sinker by Congress and the general public. There will be little or no public discussion of the plan or its long-term consequences. That's exactly what happened in 1933. Roosevelt handed Congress a bill, it was read aloud, a short discussion followed, and then it was voted on. That was hardly appropriate for a bill that laid aside the Constitution and turned our monetary system upside down. In the middle of a crisis, though, the long-term consequences were irrelevant.

A panic resulting from the millenium bug will be the chance of a lifetime for those who wish to introduce the cashless society. They know they need a crisis situation to do it, and the millenium bug presents the ideal possibility. Never will they be able to insure greater cooperation from the general public. Never will the public be more ready to lay aside its objections and play along.

Never will there be a better time to demonize those who will not go along and silence them. Those who do resist will be forced either to become outlaws and live a tenuous existence underground, or to flee from the country.

Put yourself in the shoes of the bureaucrats who want to control the population, and track every single financial transaction. You know all about the opposition there is to such ideas. You know you'll never get this carrot without a brutal fight. You know your time is running out as the old means of financing are reaching the limits of what can be done. Then along comes a millenium bug crisis. Wouldn't that be just too good an opportunity to pass up?

Of course it would!

If a crisis materializes, there will be little room for those who don't want to play the game. I've tried to make this fact perfectly clear within these pages. There may, however, be a door of hope for those of us who prefer freedom to security—a silver lining to this dark cloud approaching.

Suppose the millenium bug proves worse than most people imagine it could be. Suppose that, despite mankind's best efforts, it really does wipe out governments and businesses, starting with the most sophisticated and most highly computerized. Suppose it does destroy the world economy and the world fiat monetary system. Then the cashless society might last no more than six months or a year.

Although such a scenario would be difficult for most of us, and fatal to some, it may really turn out better in the end for those who don't care to serve money, and don't want their children and grandchildren to be slaves to a perverse system designed to narrowly define their lives and milk them for all their worth.

A Silver Lining?

If government welfare payments were to stop, and the money system came down, the country would go up in flames and the United States as we know it would cease to exist. It is possible that—at least in some parts of the country—something better might replace it.

I'm not betting on that, though. Big organizations die notoriously hard. Somehow or another, they'll survive, especially if their leaders are not afraid to turn the nation into a slave state to do it. The very fact that executive orders and laws even breach the subject should make it clear that our leaders are willing to do exactly that.

Even worse, I don't believe most Americans are ready to give up a big, intrusive government yet. Although we as a nation have sacrificed a great deal of our freedoms, and a great deal of our character to the god of money, we have not carried it through to its ultimate conclusion. We have not quite yet sold everything dear to us. And I have to realize that it may be God's intention to give us the opportunity to.

Despite such dark forebodings, there is one thing we can be certain of: No nation of slaves ever defines the future. As men are limited and defined externally, they die inside. They lose their eye for the future and seek only to drown out their present misery. And when individual men die inside, their society and their nation inevitably dies too. It may live on for a while, but no one will envy it, love it or copy it any more. Rather, people will thank God they don't live there, or under such a government. In the end it will become only a monument to the insanity, stupidity and wickedness of mankind.

Those who define the future will not be the slaves of men and money. They will be the men and women who have higher ideals, the men and women who cannot, will not and do not live by bread alone. Such will be the builders of the world to come, and they will build that world on the ashes of a fallen civilization. Whether the millenium bug incinerates that civilization in a year, or whether it falls under its own weight in 30 years by pursuing the policies that are only natural to those who worship money, it is bound to fall. This is our door of hope in a world gone crazy. Let us only be well prepared for the opportunity, lest we miss it, and lest we be counted unworthy to see that day.

Resources

The following are the resources you'll need to follow the millenium bug crisis as it develops and to prepare for it:

1. *Keeping up on the millenium bug.* Since the crisis will likely happen very fast, the best way to monitor it is through the World Wide Web. Here are some key web sites:

www.y2k.com, www.euy2k.com, www.garynorth.com, www.yardeni.com are good places to watch for news on the millenium bug. Here you can find the latest pronouncements by government figures, people in business, news reports, projections, etc.

www.bog.frb.fed.us/releases/ is where to get the latest Federal Reserve data on money supply, bank reserves, etc. This is essential data if you want to keep tabs on the possibility of a banking panic.

www.ffiec.fog/y2k offers up to date information on how the banking industry is dealing (or not dealing) with the technical side of the millenium bug.

www.logoplex.com/resources/ameagle is the website for the publisher of this book, and contains links to the above and other important sites.

2. *Historical information.* Examine some of the executive orders and laws that can be implemented in a national emergency.

>*www.fas.org/irp/offdocs/direct.htm* has the full text of various executive orders available for download.
>*afcomm.metronet.com/afc/report.html* contains the complete text of the book *War and Emergency Powers* by Gene Schroder.

2. *Personal preparedness.* These are some of the best resources on how to open a door to get out of the country if things go bad.

>***Strategic Relocation: North American Guide to Safe Places***, by Joel M. Skousen, is a book about what places in America are safest against various kinds of threats. It's a must-read if you're thinking about buying rural property or relocating.
>***Boom Counties: A Guide to Wealth and Serenity in a High-Risk Economy***, by Jack Lessinger, is another book about where to move, although it is more oriented to economic trends. Available from Socio-Economics, Box 113, Bow, WA 98232.
>***Civil War II***, by Thomas Chittum, is another important must-read book if you're seriously considering relocating. It talks about mounting racial pressures in the United States, and the likely breakup of the US into three different countries along ethnic lines. You don't want to get caught in the wrong place. Available from American Eagle Publications, Inc.
>***The Passport Report***, a book about obtaining a second passport from a different country. A second passport is an invaluable asset in times of crisis, when the one from the country you live in could be revoked without warning. Available from Scope International, Ltd., Forestside House, Rowlands Castle, Hampshire PO9 6EE, England.

Resources

Cost is $100, but well worth it. You may be entitled to a second passport somewhere already, and not even know it.

International Living Magazine discusses interesting places to visit and live overseas, overseas real estate, etc. Especially good for retirees. It is available for $58/year from Agora, Inc., 105 W. Monument St., Baltimore, MD 21201. They also offer Discovery Tours throughout the year to destinations of possible interest.

Escape from America, by Roger Gallo, a 355 page book about how to get out of the country, and what some other places are like. Very good. Available from American Eagle Publications at 1-800-719-4957, or see Gallo's website at *www.escapeartist.com*.

Getting Started in the Underground Economy, by Adam Cash, is the classic work on the undeground economy as it is today. A good starting place if you're headed underground. Get it from Loompanics, PO Box 1197, Port Townsend, WA 98368 (www.loompanics.com). They have a number of worthwhile books on the underground economy, ranging from working flea markets to running drugs.

Bartering Secrets, by Phil Hunter, is a manual on how to barter. Essential if you're going underground. Available from Wave Publications, PO Box 84902, Phoenix, AZ 85071.

Remnant Review, by Gary North. This is Gary North's monthly newsletter, and a good way to keep up on the millenium bug, albeit pricey at $99.95/year. Although I don't agree with North 100%, it's always good to listen to a variety of opinions. You can get it by writing Agora, Inc., 1217 St. Paul St., Baltimore, MD 21202.

Index

2001 A Space Oddesy	10
Agriculture, Department of	33
Air Force	21
Amish	176
amnesty	107
auto mechanic	175
backward compatibility	10
bank accounts, automated	114
Bank of America	114
Bank of Boston	57
bank run	73,80,97
banking crisis	96,101
banking emergency	101
Banking Secrecy Act	120
bankruptcy	32
beast, mark of	170
Bilderbergers	111
black market	175
Borland	18
bureaucrats	91,196
business failures	29,59
butterfly spread	62
c language	16
cash	102
cashless society	109
censorship	49
central banker, european	79
certificate of deposit	64
China	35,36
Christians	100,168
churches	170
Citibank	23,159
civil war	34
client, of media	50
Clinton, President	87
coercion	171
collapse, of government	141
compatibility test	14
computers, IRS	134
Congress	135
contracts	100,107
corporate bonds	55
cost to fix federal computers	24
cost, counting	172
Council on Foreign Relations	111
creation of money	66
credit card fraud	159
credit cards	115
credit cycle	123
crime	119,158
cryptography	165
currency	105,107,163
currency, fiat	156
date convention, european	10
debit cards	115
debt	104,124
debt, federal	121,129
debugging	26
default	128
demand account	64
demonetization	100
detention centers	153
economic collapse	131
economic models	79
economy, demonic	168
economy, underground	175
Electronic Benefits Transfer Program	117
electronic money	109
employment, without compensation	163
escape from system	153
European companies	26
exchange controls	156
executable program	18
Executive Order 12919	95,163
extremists	167
FBI	166
FDIC	56,71
Federal Reserve	58,65,99,128
Federal Reserve Notes	99
Fifth Amendment	90
FINCEN	120
fiscal year	44
food shortages	154
food stamps	32
fractional reserve banking	56,66
free markets	55
freedom	168
futures contracts	62
Gartner Group	25
God, claim to be	152
gold	90,99,101,105,122,130,163
gold clause	100
Government Accounting Office	21,26
government, cashless	116
Gross, Arthur	134
Habeas Corpus	89
IBM	14
identification systems	159
incorporated churches	170
inflation	69,104,130,140
interest calculation	12
interest rate hikes	61
interest rates	56,132,140
internet	52
intrinsic value	107

invasion	35
IRS	24,33,103,117,120,133
Japanese Americans	153
kindergarten	45
laws of prize	87
Leading Edge Computers	39
legislation, freedom-destroying	167
leverage	76
licensing	151
Lincoln, Abraham	88
Los Angeles County	24
market, captive	131
Maryland	118
Mastercard	115
McAfee, John	42
Medicare	32
Merril Lynch	23
Michelangelo	38,42
microchip	160,168
Microsoft	14
money supply	74,127
money, concept of	153
mortgage	69
Moynihan, Daniel Patrick	21
national emergency	87
National Security Agency	166
Nebraska	24
Newsweek	22,37,46
North Carolina	24
North, Gary	22,28
nuclear reactor	46
Office of Management and Budget	20
opposition	110
panic, bank	70
Paradox	13,18
passport	188
pastors	169
patriot	171
Pentium	11
police state	90
power, will to	151
press, underground	52
printing money	104
prisoners, premature release of	45
privacy	164
programmers	164
property rights	152
property taxes	176
public opinion	172
radio	170
rationing	153
rebellion, tax	154
Request for Comments, IRS	136
reserve requirements	65
reserves	74,76
resistance	108,161
restraint, fiscal	131

Revelation, book of	168
revolution	35
riots	34
risk	53,61,69
risk managers	57
Roosevelt, Franklin D.	71,88,98,195
savings account	12
secret societies	111
Secretary of Defense	20
silver coin	101
slavery	158
smart card	115,160,169
Social Security	24,32,45,133
Social Security Number	151
source code	18
Supreme Court	89
T-Bills	54
Taiwan	36
tapping phones	120
tax protesters	139
tax rate, lifetime	155
tax rates	173
tax reform	141
taxes	119,131,133,175
taxes, hidden	156
televangelists	169
television	170
terms, net 30	30
Treasury, US	117
Trilateral Commission	111
Union Pacific Railroad	23
UPS strike	98
US debt	36
USSR	158
virus, computer	42
Visa	115
Wall Street	54
War Powers Act of 1917	87,105,162
Word for Windows '97	10
World War II	92

Dr. Mark A. Ludwig is a theoretical physicist, computer systems designer and systems programmer. He received his Masters at Caltech and his Ph.D. at the University of Arizona. In addition to developing numerous products for the computer industry, he has authored several books on computer viruses and evolution. He lives in northeastern Arizona with his wife and three children.

For a catalog of important and interesting books by Mark Ludwig and other authors, write:

American Eagle Publications, Inc.
PO Box 1507
Show Low, AZ 85902

call 1-800-719-4957, or visit our Web site:

http://www.logoplex.com/resources/ameagle